Seven Wonders of the Ancient World

A Captivating Guide to the Great Pyramid of Giza, Hanging Gardens of Babylon, Temple of Artemis, Statue of Zeus, Mausoleum at Halicarnassus, and More

Free Bonus from Captivating History (Available for a Limited time)

Hi History Lovers!

Now you have a chance to join our exclusive history list so you can get your first history ebook for free as well as discounts and a potential to get more history books for free! Simply visit the link below to join.

Captivatinghistory.com/ebook

Also, make sure to follow us on Facebook, Twitter and Youtube by searching for Captivating History.

Table of Contents

Introduction

The Seven Wonders of the Ancient World are widely considered to be a testament to the ingenuity and technological advancements of ancient civilizations. Despite the fact that many of these structures no longer exist today, they continue to capture the imagination of people around the world. According to historical research, the Seven Wonders of the Ancient World were heavily influenced by Hellenistic culture and were chosen based on their grandeur and sophistication.

The Seven Wonders of the Ancient World are as follows:

- The Great Pyramid of Giza
- The Hanging Gardens of Babylon
- The Temple of Artemis
- The Statue of Zeus
- The Mausoleum of Halicarnassus
- The Colossus of Rhodes
- The Lighthouse of Alexandria

Of these, only the Great Pyramid of Giza still exists today.

Herodotus, a historian who lived from circa 484 to 425 BCE, was one of the earliest writers to document the Seven Wonders of the Ancient World. However, it is important to note that his writings may not be entirely accurate. Luckily, we don't have to take just his word for it, as other authors, such as Strabo, Diodorus, and Philo, also wrote about the ancient wonders.

According to archaeologists Peter Clayton and Martin Price, the lists of the Seven Wonders of the Ancient World were more deeply ingrained during the Renaissance period. However, it is important to note these lists were primarily based on Greek perspectives since Greek authors constituted the vast majority of writers during that era. Consequently, several regions, such as Asia, Africa, and the Americas, were excluded from the lists created in the past.

One of the Seven Wonders of the Ancient World that has been the subject of much debate is the Hanging Gardens of Babylon. Despite the fact that Herodotus, also known as the "Father of History," does not mention the Hanging Gardens of Babylon, other authors, such as Strabo and Philo, claim the gardens existed and were destroyed in an earthquake during the 1st century CE.

What happened to the other wonders? Well, the Statue of Zeus slowly fell into ruin after the Olympic Games were banned once Christianity took root. Christians saw the games as a pagan rite. As a result, Olympia, where the Statue of Zeus was located, fell into disuse. The statue was eventually taken to Constantinople, where it was destroyed in an earthquake around the 5th or 6th century CE.

The Temple of Artemis was destroyed by a mob led by Saint John Chrysostom in 401 CE, becoming yet another victim of the spread of Christianity. The Mausoleum of Halicarnassus was also affected by the religion, as it was dismantled and used by the Knights of Saint John of Rhodes (also known as the Knights Hospitaller) for their castle in Bodrum after the structure was destroyed by a series of earthquakes.

The Colossus of Rhodes was built by the Rhodians for three hundred talents and stood for fifty-six years before being destroyed. It was eventually sold to a Jewish merchant from Edessa in 654 CE. Finally, the Lighthouse of Alexandria was destroyed in 1480 after a series of earthquakes. Today, the Citadel of Qaitbay stands in its place.

But what did the Seven Wonders of the Ancient World mean to the people who saw them? This book will pull back the curtain to explore why these structures were so significant. As you explore the information in this book, you will likely come to realize why the Seven Wonders of the Ancient World still intrigue and inspire us today. After all, it is hard not to be inspired by the idea that something as great as a 455-foot-tall pyramid could happen when diverse skills and capabilities are pooled together.

Summary of events:

- c. 2550 BCE: Pharaoh Khufu (Cheops) initiated the construction of the Great Pyramid of Giza.

- c. 605–562 BCE: Legends suggest that King Nebuchadnezzar II built the Hanging Gardens of Babylon.

- c. 550 BCE: The reconstruction of the Temple of Artemis began in Ephesus.

- c. 456 BCE: The construction of the Temple of Zeus was finished.

- c. 435 BCE: Phidias created the Statue of Zeus in the Temple of Zeus at Olympia.

- c. 356 BCE: An intentional fire destroyed the Temple of Artemis at Ephesus.

- c. 323 BCE: The restoration of the Temple of Artemis occurred.

- c. 353–350 BCE: The Mausoleum of Halicarnassus, the burial place of King Mausolus of Caria, was built.

- c. 300–246 BCE: The Lighthouse of Alexandria was constructed.

- c. 292–280 BCE: The Colossus of Rhodes, a statue of Helios, stood in the harbor of Rhodes.

- c. 228 or 226 BCE: An earthquake caused the collapse of the Colossus of Rhodes.

- 262 CE: The Goths pillaged and demolished the Temple of Artemis at Ephesus.

- 395 CE: The Statue of Zeus was relocated to Constantinople.

- 401 CE: A Christian mob possibly destroyed the Temple of Artemis at Ephesus.

- 475 CE: According to Byzantine historian Zonaras, the Statue of Zeus was destroyed in a fire in Constantinople.

- c. 654 CE: Theophanes, a Byzantine historian, claimed that a Jewish merchant transported the fallen Colossus of Rhodes to Edessa to be melted down.

- 956 CE: An earthquake caused the partial collapse of the Lighthouse of Alexandria, which had previously been damaged in 950 CE.
- c. 1100 CE: After repairs, a domed mosque was added to the Lighthouse of Alexandria.
- c. 1330 CE: The Lighthouse of Alexandria ultimately collapsed due to an earthquake.
- c. 1494 CE: Portions of the Mausoleum of Halicarnassus were repurposed as walls in the Castle of Saint Peter at Bodrum by the Knights of Saint John of Rhodes.

Chapter 1 – The Great Pyramid of Giza

In the fascinating annals of Egypt's history, before the appearance of the Great Pyramid of Giza, two pivotal events stand out as profound landmarks in the evolution of pyramid construction. These events, separated by centuries, left an indelible mark on Egypt's architectural landscape and exemplify the remarkable ingenuity and vision of the ancient Egyptians.

The first of these monumental events took place during the 27th century BCE, a time when a chancellor named Imhotep lived. Imhotep was renowned for his multifaceted talents as an architect, high-ranking official, and polymath, and he graced the stage of history with an awe-inspiring creation: the Saqqara Step Pyramid.

Rising majestically in the lands of Saqqara, Egypt, this architectural marvel holds the distinction of being the first pyramid constructed in Egypt. Imhotep, driven by an unyielding desire to honor Pharaoh Djoser, embarked on an audacious endeavor to fashion a monumental structure that would transcend the boundaries of tradition.

Imhotep's brilliance shone through as he harnessed his architectural genius to fashion an unprecedented royal burial complex. The Saqqara Step Pyramid stands as a testament to Imhotep's visionary design and unwavering commitment to architectural innovation.

The architectural grandeur of the Saqqara Step Pyramid is a sight to behold. It is composed of six mastabas, rectangular structures with gently sloping sides, seamlessly stacked upon one another. Soaring to a height of approximately 205 feet (62 meters), this awe-inspiring creation was an unprecedented achievement of its time.

Centuries later, the chronicles of pyramid construction in Egypt took another momentous turn with Pharaoh Sneferu, who commissioned Egypt's first true pyramid, known as the Red Pyramid.

Nestled amidst the landscape of Dahshur, Egypt, the Red Pyramid stands as a testament to Sneferu's determination to surpass the architectural achievements of his predecessors. Its elegant and refined form with smooth, sloping sides heralded a transition from the previous step pyramid design. The Red Pyramid represents a significant milestone, an architectural turning point that would forever shape the legacy of pyramid construction in ancient Egypt. Clad in a resplendent coat of red limestone, which gave it its name, this remarkable edifice has withstood the relentless march of time, despite the removal of its original casing stones.

These two extraordinary landmarks—the Saqqara Step Pyramid and the Red Pyramid—served as the harbingers of a new era in the realm of monumental architecture in ancient Egypt. They laid the foundation for the subsequent construction of the iconic pyramids at Giza, leaving a mark on the sands of time.

Introduction to the Great Pyramid of Giza

The pyramids of Giza, which were erected during the Fourth Dynasty, stand proudly on the banks of the Nile River in northern Egypt. These magnificent structures were constructed by pharaohs who sought to honor the gods and ensure a prosperous afterlife by filling the tombs with opulent treasures. Dating back to the Old Kingdom, approximately 4,500 years ago, these remarkable constructions were built under the rule of Khufu, Khafre, and Menkaure.

Let's delve into the basic yet intriguing details of each pyramid:

1. Pharaoh Khufu: The Great Pyramid was erected around 2550 BCE. This colossal structure was meticulously assembled using a staggering 2.3 million carved stone blocks. Soaring to an initial height of 481.4 feet (146.6 meters), it reigns supreme as the largest pyramid in Egypt, captivating all who behold its grandeur.

2. Pharaoh Khafre: Nestled amidst the Giza Plateau, the pyramid belonging to Khufu's son, Khafre, is a majestic sight. Constructed between 2558 and 2532 BCE, it stands shoulder to shoulder with

the enigmatic Great Sphinx, a fascinating amalgamation of a lion's body and a pharaoh's noble countenance. This pyramid, measuring 471 feet (143.5 meters) in height, takes its place as the second-largest pyramid in Egypt.

3. Pharaoh Menkaure: Continuing the lineage of pyramid construction, Menkaure, the son of Khafre, crafted a smaller yet intricately designed pyramid sometime between 2532 and 2503 BCE. Although it is the smallest among the trio, with an original base measuring approximately 356 feet (108.5 meters) on each side and a height of about 215 feet (65.5 meters), its elegance and attention to detail make it an architectural gem in its own right.

It is important to note that the precise measurements of these pyramids vary slightly depending on the source, and there is always the potential for new discoveries that might shed more light on how tall the pyramids once were. The pyramids' heights have diminished over the centuries due to the removal of their outer casing stones, which were used for other construction projects.

The pyramids of Giza stand behind the smaller pyramids that are known as the Queen's Pyramids. From left to right: the Pyramid of Menkaure, the Pyramid of Khafre, and the Great Pyramid of Khufu.

Ricardo Liberato, CC BY-SA 2.0 <https://creativecommons.org/licenses/by-sa/2.0>, via Wikimedia Commons https://commons.wikimedia.org/wiki/File:All_Gizah_Pyramids.jpg

The Pyramid of Khufu

The Great Pyramid, also known as the Pyramid of Khufu, stands as an awe-inspiring architectural marvel in Giza, Egypt. Historical records indicate this monumental structure was completed during the reign of Khufu, the second pharaoh of the Fourth Dynasty of the Old Kingdom of Egypt. Originally towering over 481 feet (146.6 meters) in height, its current height stands at approximately 455 feet (around 139 meters) due to the loss of its exterior stone casing. Upon its completion, the Great Pyramid proudly claimed the title of the tallest structure in the world, maintaining this distinction until the construction of England's Lincoln Cathedral in 1311.

The Great Pyramid's remarkable alignment, with each side displaying an angle of approximately 51.5 degrees, stands out as one of its most notable features. This architectural masterpiece was constructed using a combination of limestone and granite, with the core composed of limestone and the exterior adorned with granite. The process of building the pyramid involved the movement and placement of over two million individual rocks.

In 2016, Egyptologist Mark Lehner and engineer Glen Dash conducted a groundbreaking study to validate a long-standing theory suggesting that the pyramid possessed a slightly lopsided appearance, with the eastern side being shorter than the western side. Employing cutting-edge technologies like laser scanning and 3D modeling, they attempted to measure the pyramid's original height. The outcome of their research uncovered fascinating insights into the vertical dimensions of the pyramid's sides. According to the study's findings, the eastern face displayed a remarkable range in original height, spanning from an impressive 755.561 to 755.817 feet (equivalent to 230.295 to 230.373 meters). The western façade fluctuated between 755.833 and 756.024 feet (approximately 230.378 and 230.436 meters). These results show that a mere 5.55 inches (or 14.1 centimeters) separated the two.

Upon entering the Great Pyramid, one would discover a total of seven boat pits distributed strategically throughout its chambers. Two pits lie on the south side, two on the east side, two are situated between the Queen's Pyramids, and one rests adjacent to the funerary temple and causeway. One of the most fascinating findings within the pyramid was the discovery of a remarkably well-preserved boat crafted from hardwood planks. Measuring around 142 feet in length, the boat's purpose and usage remain shrouded in mystery. It is likely the ship would have symbolized the barge that the sun god Ra uses to cross the sky.

Nestled southeast of the Great Pyramid are three smaller pyramids, two of which were dedicated to the wives of Khufu, namely Queen Henutsen and Queen Meritites. Another pyramid was erected in honor of Khufu's mother, Queen Hetepheres.

The Great Pyramid has three chambers. The King's Chamber is a red granite room accessed through a vast gallery. This chamber houses an empty royal sarcophagus. To safeguard the King's Chamber, an ancient mechanism was positioned in front of it, designed to deter potential burglars by lowering massive blocks in their path. Despite these protective measures, the chamber was ultimately subjected to theft.

An entrance measuring fifty-nine feet grants access to the northern part of the pyramid. The entrance leads to a downward-sloping corridor connecting to an unfinished underground room. Situated at the heart of the pyramid lies the Queen's Chamber, which is accessible through the descending corridor and linked to the burial chamber, also known as the King's Chamber.

The purpose of the Queen's Chamber has long been a topic of debate among Egyptologists. While the traditional belief suggests that the chamber was intended for the burial of a queen, recent research has cast doubt on this assumption. The chamber's design closely resembles the subterranean chamber beneath the pyramid, yet its true purpose remains uncertain.

The air shafts in the King's and Queen's Chambers have also been a subject of contention among researchers. Egyptian archaeologist Zahi Hawass states that the air shafts in the Queen's Chamber extend quite far but eventually reach a dead end. Conversely, Egyptologist Miroslav Verner argues that the air shafts in the King's Chamber lead outside the pyramid, proposing that they might even lead to Khufu's actual burial chamber since his sarcophagus was empty when it was explored in the late 18th century. Hawass further notes that the Great Pyramid stands apart from the other pyramids in Egypt due to its door featuring copper handles, igniting speculation about potential concealed secrets.

Recent research has employed muon imaging. Muons are high-energy particles that continually descend upon Earth, and they are used to probe the internal structure of the Great Pyramid of Giza. By utilizing this method, researchers have identified a sizable void situated above the pyramid's Grand Gallery, a lengthy corridor linking the King's Chamber and the Queen's Chamber. This void spans approximately ninety-eight feet in length and twenty feet in height. The research also unveiled evidence of a smaller secondary void beyond the pyramid's northern face.

It is vital to acknowledge that this research is in its preliminary stages, necessitating further investigation to unveil the precise nature and purpose of these voids. The discovery of these enigmatic spaces has ignited immense interest and triggered spirited debates among scholars, but their exact purpose and contents continue to elude us.

It is commonly acknowledged that the construction of the Pyramid of Khufu demanded an immense amount of time and labor. Estimates suggest that over 230 cubic meters of stone were laid daily throughout Khufu's approximate thirty-year reign (he ruled anywhere from twenty-three years to sixty-three years).

The social status of the workers involved in building the Great Pyramid remains a subject of debate among scholars. It was once commonly accepted that the pyramids were built using slave labor. However, many historians argue against the notion that these workers were slaves, citing the Diary of Merer as evidence to support their claim. This ancient Egyptian logbook provides detailed accounts of the transportation of limestone from Tura to Giza during the pyramid's construction. The logbook depicts a well-organized workforce led by a supervisor who was responsible for efficiently transporting materials across significant distances.

However, it is important to note that the logbook does not offer direct evidence of this crew's involvement in constructing the Great Pyramid specifically. Nevertheless, the information within the logbook suggests the workers who dedicated themselves to building the pyramids were not slaves but highly skilled laborers.

Recent studies on the construction of the Great Pyramid of Giza have shed light on the diverse materials used to create it. These materials include limestone sourced from the Tura quarry in Egypt and cedarwood imported from Lebanon. The successful transportation of these materials across vast distances stands as a testament to the logistical and organizational capabilities of the ancient Egyptians.

The Pyramid of Khufu is the largest of the three main pyramids at Giza.

The Pyramid of Khafre

The Great Pyramid of Giza is the pyramid that is listed as one of the Seven Wonders of the Ancient World. However, it is worth delving into the background of the other pyramids at Giza since they are all awe-inspiring. When Khufu, the father of Khafre, passed away, Khafre did not immediately succeed him. Instead, Khafre's older brother, Djedefre, ascended the throne and constructed his own pyramid at Abu Rawash, located about five miles north of Giza. Sadly, the passage of time has left the pyramid mostly in ruins.

Djedefre ruled Egypt for approximately ten to fourteen years before his demise, leading to Khafre assuming the throne. Khafre returned to Giza and set out to erect his pyramid, which originally towered at a height of 471 feet. Today, it stands at around 448 feet. Though slightly smaller in size than the Pyramid of Khufu, the Pyramid of Khafre appears taller due to its elevated location and the use of unique construction materials.

Unlike the Pyramid of Khufu, which featured a limestone casing, the Pyramid of Khafre employed a combination of red granite for the lower levels and limestone for the upper levels. This stark contrast in materials gives the Pyramid of Khafre an unmistakable appearance, making it appear larger than the Pyramid of Khufu.

Moreover, the satellite pyramid adjacent to the Pyramid of Khafre showcases a simpler structure compared to its counterpart. With two entrances—one at the ground level and another positioned thirty-eight feet above the pyramid's base—this design indicates the builders' intentions to streamline the internal structure, perhaps to avoid the challenges encountered during the construction of the Pyramid of Khufu. Passageways interconnect the entrances, leading to the burial chamber, which now contains an empty red granite sarcophagus. The absence of mummies or relics within the chamber suggests that it may have fallen victim to theft in ancient times.

The statue of Khafre, currently exhibited at the Egyptian Museum in Cairo, stands as one of ancient Egypt's most significant surviving sculptures. The statue depicts the king seated on a throne and bears hieroglyphs that symbolize Khafre's duty to rule Egypt as a unified state.

The Pyramid of Khafre at Giza. If you see a picture of all three pyramids together, you might think the middle pyramid is the tallest, but the Pyramid of Khafre was actually constructed on slightly higher ground.

The Pyramid of Menkaure

The Pyramid of Menkaure is the smallest of the pyramids at Giza, but it is by no means insignificant. Extensive studies reveal that this extraordinary structure boasts a base measuring 356 feet (108.5 meters) on each side, with a height of 215 feet (65.5 meters). However, such dimensions pale in comparison to the colossal Pyramid of Khufu, the largest of the three pyramids.

What sets the Pyramid of Menkaure apart are the intriguing additions adorning its southern side: three smaller pyramids, often referred to as satellite pyramids. These enigmatic structures, though diminutive in scale, contribute to the mystique and allure of the Pyramid of Menkaure.

Venturing further within the pyramid's interior, one encounters an intricate network of passages, leading intrepid explorers to an antechamber and a sacred burial chamber. The entrance to this hallowed edifice lies nestled at a low level, barely above the ground's surface, tempting seekers of knowledge to unveil the secrets hidden within.

Archaeologists discovered a sarcophagus with human bones within the Pyramid of Menkaure. This remarkable find was attributed to the renowned British soldier and Egyptologist Howard Vyse, who, in the 19th century, made an indelible mark on our understanding of Egypt's past.

However, fate dealt a cruel blow to this sarcophagus, as tragedy struck during its journey to England. In an unfortunate turn of events, the vessel entrusted with its safe passage, the *Beatrice*, succumbed to the whims of the treacherous sea, capsizing in 1838. The once-magnificent sarcophagus, destined to grace the halls of scholarly inquiry, met a tragic end, lost to the depths of the ocean.

This sarcophagus was not Menkaure's final resting place, as the sarcophagus held the bones of a woman. His coffin also had human bones in them, but testing revealed they were not old enough to be his. You can see the lid of his coffin in the British Museum today.

The reduced scale of the Pyramid of Menkaure, at least when compared to the grandeur of its counterparts, continues to baffle scholars. The reasons behind this architectural disparity have ignited heated debates among experts, each proposing their own theories to unravel the mysteries of the past. Some conjecture that the confines of the Giza Plateau left little room for the construction of another grand pyramid, while others delve into the realm of politics and economics, suggesting that Menkaure's reign was plagued by issues that prevented the construction of a larger pyramid.

As we tread upon the hallowed grounds of these awe-inspiring structures, the echoes of a lost era beckon us, urging us to unravel the perplexing secrets of the past.

The Pyramid of Menkaure was the third and smallest pyramid built at Giza.

The Great Sphinx

The Sphinx held a revered position as the steadfast guardian of the pyramids and the pharaohs interred within their sacred confines. It embodied the pharaoh's unwavering power and indomitable strength, a resplendent symbol woven into the tapestry of the Giza Plateau.

Interestingly, the term "sphinx," a name of Greek origin, carries a duality of meaning, hinting at both the notion of a "strangler" and the concept of being "constricted." Curiously enough, the Egyptians did not employ this particular appellation. Instead, depictions of the sphinx can be found in diverse artworks scattered across the ancient Middle East, Greece, and even India, forging a connection that spans continents and civilizations.

The Great Sphinx, in particular, assumes the form of a mythical creature, melding the regal countenance of a pharaoh with the commanding body of a lion. Legend intertwines itself with history, as some say that the face of the Great Sphinx bears an uncanny resemblance to Pharaoh Khafre, who is often regarded as its illustrious creator. However, a parallel narrative exists, proposing that Djedefre, in an act of filial reverence, constructed the monument in homage to his father.

The origin of the Sphinx traces back to the very bedrock of the Giza Plateau, as ancient architects hewed and shaped its enduring form with unwavering determination. Successive generations contributed layers upon layers of limestone blocks to restore the monument's weathered façade. However, as the years passed, the Great Sphinx bore witness to the ravages of time, suffering the loss of its once-proud nose, an enigma that has intrigued countless minds throughout the centuries.

Within the realm of lore, a tale once flourished suggesting that Napoleon Bonaparte, in a moment of audacious conquest, fired a fateful shot that severed the nose from its sculpted face. Yet, the brushstrokes of historical truth render this narrative a mere tale, for paintings predating the French invasion depict the Sphinx in its impaired state. Another popular account recounts the actions of a Sufi Muslim who became disenchanted by the locals' veneration of the Sphinx. This man defaced the monument, fervently believing that no image should be worshiped.

The exact circumstances of how the nose was damaged remain shrouded in uncertainty. Archaeological investigations indicate that its disappearance occurred sometime between the 3rd and 10th centuries CE, likely succumbing to the relentless forces of weathering and erosion.

A colossal entity, the Great Sphinx has a staggering length of approximately 240 feet (73 meters). During the annual spring equinox, a celestial spectacle unfolds, as the radiant sun descends majestically over the Sphinx's broad shoulder, casting an ethereal glow upon it.

The Great Sphinx located in front of the Pyramid of Giza in Egypt.

Materials That Were Used to Build the Pyramids of Giza

The pyramids of Egypt stand as testaments to human ingenuity and architectural prowess. These remarkable structures, which are considered among the most impressive achievements in history, were constructed with a range of materials and techniques.

R. O. Faulkner, an esteemed English Egyptologist, shed light on the widespread use of limestone in pyramid construction. This versatile stone, with its fine texture and remarkable properties, served as the backbone and outer façade of the pyramids. The inner causeways and wall coatings featured white limestone obtained from locales like the Mokattam Hills, near modern-day Cairo.

Transporting the rough limestone cores posed a formidable challenge. Local quarries provided the necessary supplies, but for the coveted white limestone used, the Egyptians had to venture further. Delving deep into the earth, they meticulously excavated tunnels, plunging up to 160 feet below the surface. The resulting blocks were meticulously cut into smaller pieces. These blocks would be loaded onto sleds that animals or perhaps men dragged through the sand. It is also possible that blocks were loaded onto ships.

While limestone prevailed as the principal material of the ancient pyramids, the Egyptians also used pink granite and basalt. Pink granite, renowned for its durability and aesthetic allure, was a rarity found only in select southern Egyptian locations. The arduous journey from the quarries at Aswan brought this prized stone to construction sites. Similarly, basalt, known as alabaster, occasionally graced the pyramid floors. It was extracted from open pits or hidden underground deposits.

Mud bricks played a significant role in pyramid construction as well. Blending mud and water, the Egyptians fashioned these bricks into a rectangular shape, baking them in the sun's warm embrace. As the rays warmed the bricks, they solidified into a resilient form. To further enhance their durability, the bricks went into an oven.

Through their masterful use of various materials, the ancient Egyptians triumphed over the limitations of their era. Even though they didn't have advanced technology, they were able to overcome their limitations and create structures that could truly pass the test of time.

The Construction of the Pyramids

The pyramids have fascinated people for centuries, but in many ways, they are still shrouded in mystery. The pyramids at Giza, for instance, showcase remarkable technological achievements that continue to astound archaeologists and academics.

According to the accounts of Herodotus, an ancient Greek historian, the construction of the pyramids might have required a staggering 20 years and the labor of 100,000 individuals. However, more recent research suggests a smaller workforce of approximately twenty thousand workers and support staff who managed to complete the construction within two decades. Excavations in the vicinity have unearthed evidence suggesting that the workers were well nourished and supported by the government, with resources likely procured from other Egyptian cities as part of a national endeavor to demonstrate wealth and power.

Historical records indicate that the responsibility of selecting the ideal construction site for the pyramid, as well as managing the personnel and resources, fell upon the vizier, the second highest-ranking official in Egypt. Hemiunu, believed to be Khufu's nephew and the mastermind behind the design and construction of the Great Pyramid, likely acquired his technical expertise from his father, Nefermaat, who was Khufu's brother. The choice of Giza as the location for the pyramids was based on the plateau's ability to support the weight of these colossal structures, as pyramids built on sand would deteriorate more rapidly.

While extensive evidence in the form of bills, logbooks, letters, and articles suggests the completion of the Great Pyramid happened during Khufu's reign, the explicit details regarding its construction are scant. Numerous theories and recent findings provide different explanations for the construction process, yet the knowledge and specialized equipment required to build the Great Pyramid according to its precise design continue to pose a significant barrier to understanding its creation.

One prevalent theory proposes the use of ramps. A ramp would have been constructed around the base of the pyramid and progressively elevated alongside its construction. However, this theory encounters various challenges, including the scarcity of wood in Egypt, rendering the construction of numerous ramps implausible. Moreover, the angle at which the workers would have needed to push the stones upward appears physically impossible without the aid of something akin to a modern-day crane.

French architect Jean-Pierre Houdin put forth a modified ramp hypothesis, suggesting that the ramps were situated inside the pyramid. According to his theory, the ramps would have been used for the pyramid's exterior during the initial stages of construction, with the structure's interior being completed at the same time. The stones transported from the quarry would have been carried up the ramps to their designated spots. This explanation could account for the presence of shafts within the pyramid, but it fails to address the labor requirements or the immense mass of the stones.

Another intriguing theory posits the use of hydraulic power. The high water table beneath the Giza Plateau, where the pyramids stand, is believed to have played a crucial role in this. The Egyptians employed a tool called a shaduf, consisting of a long pole with a bucket, a rope, and a counterweight, to extract water from wells. It is hypothesized that the hydraulic force from below, in combination with hoists situated above, could have been employed to move the stones within the pyramid.

Renowned Egyptologist Zahi Hawass confirmed the challenges posed by the high water table during excavations. Geological studies indicate that the Giza Plateau and its surroundings were more agriculturally inclined during the Old Kingdom since the water table was higher. Thus, it is plausible that the Giza laborers would have constructed the pyramid more efficiently by harnessing the force of the high water table rather than relying on external ramps or other means.

Regardless of the diverse hypotheses proposed, the alignment of the southeastern tips of the three pyramids, alongside the presence of mortuary temples and causeways connecting them, stands as a testament to the high level of planning and organizational capabilities employed during the construction process.

Who Were the Builders of the Pyramids?

Recent scholarly research challenges the widely accepted notion that Hebrew slaves were involved in the construction of the pyramids at Giza, as there is no concrete evidence to support this assumption. While some have turned to the Book of Exodus for support, ancient records do not substantiate the claim that Hebrew slaves were present in ancient Egypt.

Ancient Egyptians held the belief that civic duty and participation in the construction of public monuments, including pyramids, temples, and cemeteries, were essential in honoring the pharaoh and the gods. Therefore, it is believed that the government hired farmers and other laborers to work on these structures during the annual flooding of the Nile River. The Nile's annual flooding, a vital aspect of Egyptian life, deposited fertile soil across the coastal agricultural areas. However, this flooding rendered farming impossible, prompting the government to employ these farmers in other projects. These laborers were responsible for transporting stones and erecting obelisks, temples, and pyramids.

Archaeological excavations shed light on the working conditions of employees involved in the construction of the Pyramid of Giza. These workers received exceptional medical care, had access to food supplies, and consumed approximately four thousand pounds of meat daily, sourced from sheep, goats, and calves. This is supported by the abundance of animal remains discovered in the area. Additionally, the skeletal remains of laborers found in tombs exhibit signs of dental work and expert repair, further substantiating the notion that these workers were well-cared for.

Overseers were employed to supervise the construction process. While documentation regarding the education and knowledge of these overseers is limited, they were tasked with managing the workforce and ensuring the completion of projects to a high standard.

By analyzing this research, it becomes apparent that the construction of the pyramids at Giza did not rely on Hebrew slaves, contrary to popular assumption. Instead, the involvement of farmers and laborers, who were provided with favorable working conditions, seems more likely.

The Great Pyramid as a Tomb

The construction of the Great Pyramid, which is one of the most iconic and well-known structures in the world, was a monumental undertaking. The ancient Egyptians believed the pharaohs needed a grand tomb to serve as a bridge between the gods and the mortals.

Ancient Egyptians were deeply concerned about the welfare of the soul in the afterlife, and this can be observed in the tombs that have been discovered in Egypt, from the simplest to the most extravagant, such as the tomb of Tutankhamun. These tombs have given us extensive evidence, such as engravings and paintings. The Pyramid Texts were funerary texts found in the pyramids of the pharaohs, and they were very prominent during the Old Kingdom. These texts were essentially spells that helped ease people's transition to the afterlife.

Despite the Great Pyramid's grandeur, there has been some debate over whether it was actually used as a tomb. This argument is based on the fact that no mummies or grave goods have yet been discovered. However, it is important to note that grave robbery has been a documented problem in Egypt for centuries.

Egyptologists suggest that the pyramid was looted for artifacts as early as the New Kingdom (c. 1570-1069 BCE), possibly due to the declining importance of Giza as a royal necropolis and the preference for the Valley of the Kings as the favored burial ground for pharaohs.

This does not mean that Giza was completely overlooked during the New Kingdom. There is evidence that pharaohs, such as Ramesses II, better known as Ramesses the Great (r. 1279-1213 BCE), had a keen interest in the area. Rameses II, an influential pharaoh, displayed his reverence for the majestic Great Sphinx by erecting a modest temple right before it. However, his fourth son, Khaemweset, embarked on a mission to safeguard and preserve this sacred site for future generations. Khaemweset, who is hailed as the world's first Egyptologist, dedicated his life to unraveling the secrets of Giza, tirelessly documenting, meticulously restoring, and fervently safeguarding these ancient monuments from the ravages of time.

Herodotus wrote that the Great Pyramid had been looted in the 5th century BCE. In more recent times, visitors can access the pyramid via the so-called "Robbers Tunnel," which was supposedly constructed around 820 CE by Caliph al-Ma'mum in an attempt to gain access to the wealth hidden inside. Throughout history, tomb raiders have frequently targeted the pyramid, and it is likely that any valuables that might have been present during Khufu's and his immediate successors' rule were removed at some point.

While the debate over the purpose of the Great Pyramid continues, it is clear that the ancient Egyptians placed great importance on the construction of grand tombs for their pharaohs. The Great Pyramid, which is the largest tomb of all, was likely believed to serve as the pharaoh's eternal home in the afterlife. The fact that grave goods and mummies have not been discovered within the pyramid should not necessarily be taken as evidence that the pyramid was not used as a tomb.

Mummification in Ancient Egypt

Pyramids and mummies are likely the first things to come to mind for many people when discussing ancient Egypt. The close association between these two elements is not incidental since mummies were frequently entombed in pyramids. The ancient Egyptians held the belief that mummification was intimately connected with the afterlife and the rebirth of the body. This belief was based on their observations of natural phenomena, such as the sun's movements and the life cycles seen in grains and lunar phases.

Ancient Egyptians believed that as long as there was order and the proper requirements were met, the body would be able to survive in the afterlife.

The Pyramid Texts, which date back to the Old Kingdom, suggest that mummification was seen as a necessary process for preserving the body. Based on these texts, chaos engulfed the cosmos when the deity of the underworld, Osiris, met his demise. The essential components for embalming his body, such as resin, incense, and honey, were said to have been formed from the tears shed by the gods.

Before the development of mummification techniques, the bodies of the deceased were simply thrown into pits and covered with sand in the hopes that the dry desert climate would aid in preserving them. However, as burial practices became more elaborate, with the use of mud brick linings and wooden coffins, the bodies began to deteriorate rapidly. To counteract this, the internal organs were removed, and the body was treated with mummifying substances.

Mummification was a common practice from 2400 BCE to the Greco-Roman era. By the time of the Ptolemaic dynasty (the last ruling dynasty of Egypt), mummification had become affordable for most people. Initially, it was believed that only pharaohs could achieve eternal life through mummification, but by 2000 BCE, it was thought that anyone could access the afterlife as long as their body was properly mummified and the necessary objects were buried with them.

However, this was a luxury that was only affordable to the wealthy. The poor would still be mummified, but the process was much simpler. The very poor would be buried in the hot desert sands, which would dry out their body. The body would be covered with natron, a combination of something called soda ash and baking soda, and then covered with some wrappings. The body would be buried in a shallow grave with some personal objects. In the early days, most commoners could not afford to be mummified.

As the mummification process evolved, natron became the primary substance for drying out corpses. The bodies of the elite were tightly wrapped in linen and left for thirty-five to forty days to dry out fully. The internal organs were extracted, treated with dry natron, and carefully stored within canopic jars. These containers were safeguarded by the four sons of the deity Horus. After thoroughly dehydrating the body, it was filled with sawdust, lichen, mud sourced from the Nile, and fragments of cloth to enhance its flexibility. The face was covered with a mask, and the body was further adorned with amulets and other funerary items.

It should be noted that the mummification process was not a requirement for resurrection in the afterlife, but it was widely believed to be the best course of action. Prayers from the *Book of the Dead*, a funerary text popular in the New Kingdom, were often used to help guide the deceased to the next life.

The Arabic term *mumiya*, which means bitumen, is where the English word "mummification" originates. Bitumen, a type of pitch, was used in the early stages of preservation in the Late Period.

Mummification was an important aspect of ancient Egyptian culture and belief, with the process evolving over time. The primary substances used in mummification were sawdust, lichen, beeswax, resin, natron, onions, Nile mud, and frankincense. The body was cleaned and wrapped in as many as thirty-five layers of linen before being submerged in resins and oils, which gave the skin a pitch-black appearance. If the deceased came from a poor family, their family would provide the funeral cloth, which was typically made from old bedsheets or used clothing. The organs were removed, and the cranial cavity was filled with resins via a funnel. The face was oftentimes masked, either with cartonnage (a plaster made from papyrus and water) or gold and silver, the latter of which was mainly reserved for royalty.

Embalmers used a specific set of tools during the mummification process. These instruments consisted of an oil jar, a funnel, bronze rods with hooks for extracting the brain, an embalmer's knife for making an incision in the abdomen, and a wooden tool resembling an adze, used to remove the internal organs. These items were often left in the tomb or nearby once the process was complete[1]. The end goal of mummification

---

[1] There isn't a definitive answer as to why the embalmers left their tools behind. However, it's possible that they left them as offerings to the gods or as a way to aid the deceased in the afterlife. The items could also have been left as a sign of respect for the dead or as a way to commemorate the mummification process. It's also possible that the items were simply left behind due to practical reasons, such as the difficulty of transporting them out of the tomb.

was to preserve the body for the afterlife, as it was believed that the soul would return to the body. Mummification was a long and complex process, but it was considered a sacred duty and an essential aspect of society in ancient Egypt.

Abandonment and Discovery

Between the years 2181 and 2040 BCE, during the First Intermediate Period, Giza was deserted and gradually deteriorated until the Middle Kingdom (approximately 2040–1782 BCE) era. The rulers of the Middle Kingdom vandalized and looted temples, tombs, and pyramids, claiming sculptures for their own construction endeavors. However, during the period of the New Kingdom pharaohs (1570–1069 BCE), a shift occurred, as they devoted themselves to the restoration of Giza.

In 30 BCE, Rome conquered Egypt after the Battle of Actium, and the reverence of the Great Pyramid of Giza and other smaller pyramids, temples, buildings, and tombs were lost. The site remained mostly disregarded until Napoleon's Egyptian campaign, which lasted from 1798 to 1801. Napoleon was interested in the legends of the pharaohs, so he dispatched a team of academics and scientists to catalog the monuments and culture of ancient Egypt. Napoleon's efforts led to a large number of tourists being drawn to Egypt, which, in turn, prompted more people to conduct research and excavations.

British archaeologist Sir William Matthew Flinders Petrie is primarily responsible for the pyramids of Giza's excavation, as he provided a detailed and accurate survey of the pyramids in the early 1880s. His efforts laid the groundwork for all subsequent excavations, and he took great care to ensure the historical accuracy of the artifacts he discovered. His desire to learn everything about the Great Pyramid without endangering the structure established rules to protect and maintain Egypt's historic monuments. It might shock you to learn this, but archaeologists in the 19th century did quite a bit of damage to the sites they explored. They used dynamite and other methods that are frowned upon today.

Archaeological discoveries, even those that damaged the sites, revealed the grandeur and magnificence of the ancient Egyptian civilization's craftsmanship, such as the empty sarcophagus of a queen adorned with furniture and jewelry. Additionally, the presence of mastabas, flat-roofed structures often found in royal tombs that were organized in a grid pattern around the pyramids, suggests the site was a thriving social and commercial center, with artifacts potentially moved to Giza from other parts of ancient Egypt and the eastern Mediterranean. These findings suggest that the focus of study should not be solely on how the pharaohs died but also on how they lived. The pyramids and the hieroglyphics written on the walls of the tombs provide insight into the languages and cultures of the past.

Using 21ˢᵗ-century Technology to Bring the Dead Back to Life

In recent years, advancements in technology have allowed for non-invasive examinations of mummified remains. By utilizing equipment like CT scans, MRIs, X-rays, and endoscopic cameras, researchers are able to gain detailed information about the mummies without causing any damage to the remains. This has allowed for a greater understanding of the mummification process and provides information about the person's gender, age, general health, and method of mummification. Furthermore, analysis of the soft tissue extracted from the mummies has revealed important biological details, such as DNA, genetic markers, and disorders.

Summary of Events

- 27ᵗʰ century BCE: The Saqqara Step Pyramid for Pharaoh Djoser was designed by Imhotep. It was the first pyramid built in Egypt.

- c. 2575-2551 BCE: Pharaoh Sneferu constructed Egypt's first true pyramid, known as the Red Pyramid.

- c. 2550 BCE: The Great Pyramid of Giza was completed by Pharaoh Khufu (also known as Cheops by the Greeks).

- c. 2558-2532 BCE: The second pyramid complex at Giza, the Pyramid of Khafre, was completed.

- c. 2532-2503 BCE: The third pyramid complex at Giza, the Pyramid of Menkaure, was constructed.

Chapter 2 – The Hanging Gardens of Babylon

<u>Babylon, the Gates of the Gods</u>

"When the lofty Anu, King of the Anunnaki, and Bel, lord of heaven and earth, he who determines the destiny of the land, committed the rule of all mankind to Marduk, the chief son of Ea; when they made him great among the Igigi; when they pronounced the lofty name of Babylon; when they made it famous among the quarters of the world and in its midst established an everlasting kingdom whose foundations were firm as heaven and earth – at that time, Anu and Bel called me, Hammurabi, the exalted prince, the worshiper of the gods, to cause justice to prevail in the land, to go forth like the Sun over the Black Head Race, to enlighten the land."

-The Code of Hammurabi

The Code of Hammurabi holds immense historical importance. Hammurabi, the sixth monarch of the Amorite dynasty, governed Babylon from 1792 to 1750 BCE, displaying his dominance as the ruler of Sumeria, Acadia, and the surrounding territories. During his reign, the city-state of Babylon underwent a remarkable transformation, evolving into a formidable empire that encompassed Mesopotamia. Its vast territories stretched from Kurdistan to the Persian Gulf. Babylon's dominance even surpassed that of the formidable Assyrian capital of Nineveh.

In ancient Sumeria, Babylon was renowned as Ka-dingirra, the revered "Gateway of the Gods." According to biblical accounts, it was established by Nimrod, who was the descendant of Cush, the grandson of Ham, and the great-grandson of Noah. The city's gates, named after deities like Shamash, Ishtar, Marduk, Adad, Enlil, Zababa, and Uresh, served as a testament to its rich spiritual heritage. The construction of the legendary Ishtar Gate took place during the reign of Nebuchadnezzar II, the second king of the Chaldean dynasty. This colossal entryway led to the sanctuary of Marduk and served as a fortified enclosure controlling the passage to the northern part of the city. It also housed one of the Seven Wonders of the Ancient World: the Hanging Gardens of Babylon, which were commissioned for Amytis, the queen consort of Nebuchadnezzar II.

Shifting back to the era of Hammurabi, the Amorite ruler left behind a legal legacy known as the Code of Hammurabi. This ancient legal code was likely influenced by earlier law codes, including those of Ur-Nammu, Eshnunna, Bilalama, and Lipit-Ishtar of Isin. Inscribed on a towering stele that stood at a height of eight feet, the code consisted of three hundred laws. Adorning the top of the stele is a bas-relief depicting the sun god Shamash delivering the laws to Hammurabi. Below this intricate portrayal are the laws themselves, inscribed in Akkadian cuneiform script. They encompassed a broad spectrum of subjects, including the establishment of equitable pricing and remuneration, civil and judicial protocols, and penalties for various transgressions.

Regrettably, the stele encountered chaos. Around 1200 BCE, Babylon suffered from looting during invasions led by the neighboring kingdom of Elam. The Code of Hammurabi was taken as a trophy to the city of Susa by King Shutruk-Nakhunte. It remained hidden until its rediscovery in December 1901 by a French archaeological expedition. The stele was then transported to Paris, where it currently resides in the Louvre Museum. Its presence there serves as a testament to the wisdom and legal systems of ancient times.

In the early 20th century, archaeological excavations of Babylon's ruins began. Between 1902 and 1914, German archaeologists conducted extensive digs that unearthed remnants of the magnificent Ishtar Gate. The fragments discovered were transported to Berlin, where a meticulous reconstruction of the gate took place within the Pergamon Museum. Today, visitors have the opportunity to marvel at the restored Ishtar Gate, which is an example of the grandeur and architectural accomplishments of the ancient Babylonian civilization.

Introduction: The Hanging Gardens of Babylon

The Ishtar Gate was not the only magnificent structure created during the Babylonian Empire. According to Greek poets, the Hanging Gardens of Babylon were constructed by King Nebuchadnezzar II around 600 BCE near the Euphrates River (modern-day Iraq). The monument, which may have reached a height of seventy-five to eighty feet, was built primarily to appease the king's beloved wife, Amytis, because she missed her beautiful home in Media (western Iran).

Another legend suggests that Queen Sammu-ramat (Semiramis in Greek), who ruled circa 811 to 806 BCE, may have built the gardens, which were possibly located on the rooftop of the palace. A study conducted between the 20th and 21st centuries argues that the Hanging Gardens may have thrived on rooftops or terraced ziggurats. However, scholars aren't sure who exactly built the gardens; some believe they never even existed.

There are no extant Babylonian records that discuss the Hanging Gardens. However, there are early accounts of the gardens, although there is no evidence that these writers saw the wonder with their own eyes. The earliest written account of the Hanging Gardens of Babylon comes from Berossus, a Babylonian priest who recorded his thoughts around 290 BCE. Later, Greek writers, such as Strabo and Diodorus Siculus, both of whom were active during the 1st century BCE and possibly the 1st century CE, also mentioned the gardens. Even though the gardens were written about many centuries after Nebuchadnezzar's reign and by individuals who may or may not have visited Babylon, various accounts describe the Hanging Gardens as if the author were there. For instance, the geographer Strabo (c. 64 BCE–c. 23 CE) represented the gardens as being close to the Euphrates and flowing through Babylon.[2]

Diodorus Siculus claims that the terraces reached heights of sixty-five feet and sloped upward, showcasing an old auditorium. There are reports of vast gardens documented in Mesopotamia before Babylon was believed to house the gardens if they even existed in the first place.

---

[2] It is unclear whether the gardens flowed through Babylon or if this is referring to the river. The description given by Strabo only mentions that the gardens were near the Euphrates and flowed through Babylon but does not provide further details.

Furthermore, some academics argue that the Hanging Gardens were not built by Nebuchadnezzar II but by King Sennacherib of Assyria (r. 704–681 BCE) in Nineveh rather than Babylon. These scholars believe that the idea that the Hanging Gardens were in Babylon was a major error, as historical discoveries have revealed that Nineveh was known as "Old Babylon" and was a major center of Mesopotamian civilization before the rise of Babylon.

In fact, Sennacherib was known to have built a personal garden in Nineveh that was considered one of the wonders of the ancient world. Some historians speculate that the stories of the Hanging Gardens might have been inspired by Sennacherib's garden and that later writers mistakenly attributed them to Babylon.

The location of the Hanging Gardens of Babylon remains unknown, but many believe they could have been found on or near the east bank of the Euphrates River, about thirty-one miles (fifty kilometers) south of present-day Baghdad in Iraq. However, this is only a theory, as the gardens have only been described in ancient Greek and Roman literature. Some speculate that the gardens were a product of the imagination of Greek intellectuals and poets, while others believe they were a nostalgically imagined oasis for warriors returning from battle.

Despite the lack of concrete evidence for the existence of the Hanging Gardens, the legend continues to capture the imagination of people around the world. Whether they were a real architectural wonder or simply a product of someone's fantasy, the Hanging Gardens of Babylon remain one of the most enduring and intriguing mysteries of the ancient world.

An illustration of the Hanging Gardens of Babylon by the Dutch artist Martin Heemskerck in the 16ᵗʰ century CE.
https://www.worldhistory.org/image/77/hanging-gardens-of-babylon/

Who Was Nebuchadnezzar II?

During the reign of Hammurabi (r. 1792–1750 BCE), the Babylonian Empire rose to prominence and dominated the towns of Mesopotamia. The first iteration of the Babylonian Empire eventually fell around 1595 BCE with the rise of the Persians. Under the leadership of Nabopolassar (626–605 BCE), the Neo-Babylonian Empire was formed. This empire would expand into new territories and create amazing works of art, particularly in regard to architecture.

According to historical accounts, King Nebuchadnezzar II ruled over the empire from 605 to 562 BCE. It is believed that Babylon, located in modern-day Iraq, was a vast and productive city situated between the Tigris and Euphrates Rivers. Since the Neo-Assyrian Empire had been laid to waste, with the capital of Assyria, Nineveh, being overrun during Nabopolassar's reign, Nebuchadnezzar II was able to focus on training a large and powerful army and constructing war chariots, which allowed him to take control of a significant number of territories.

Nebuchadnezzar II demanded taxes from all his subjects, which was (and still is) a common practice. Around 600 BCE, the king of Judah refused to pay any more taxes to Babylon. In 598, King Nebuchadnezzar II attacked Jerusalem, setting in motion the infamous Babylonian captivity. This event is probably what Nebuchadnezzar II is most remembered for, as many Judaeans became captives of Babylon. Jerusalem was ultimately destroyed after a thirty-month siege, and the Great Temple was razed to the ground.

Despite these violent acts, the Book of Daniel reveals that during Nebuchadnezzar II's reign, Babylon flourished and became the most beautiful city in the world. This was achieved through the construction of enormous palaces and temples, as well as structures known as ziggurats, which were believed to have been used as places of worship.

The Appearance of the Gardens in Historical Works

The Hanging Gardens of Babylon remain a mystery in terms of its origin and construction. However, by studying the accounts of early historians, such as Diodorus Siculus, Strabo, and Philo of Byzantium, a glimpse into the gardens can be obtained. It must be emphasized again that there is no proof these historians actually witnessed the gardens firsthand, but the records are important since they are the only proof we have that the gardens might have existed.

According to Diodorus Siculus, a Greek historian, the entrance to the Hanging Gardens was sloped in a manner similar to a hillside and consisted of multiple tiers, each with its own unique components, increasing in size from tier to tier. The gardens were said to have been constructed with earth piled up on each tier and covered with trees of varying sizes and shapes, providing a mesmerizing spectacle for those who viewed it. Furthermore, it was said that the gardens had water mechanisms in place to draw an adequate supply of water from the river, although the inner workings of these mechanisms were not observable.

Another Greek historian, Strabo, described the size of the gardens as quadrangular, with four plethra (one plethron was equal to one hundred Greek feet) along each side. The foundations of the gardens were cube-like and constructed with vaults that had arched openings. Stairs were used to ascend to the roof terrace.

An engineer and writer named Philo of Byzantium also wrote about the Seven Wonders of the Ancient World. He questioned whether the plants in the Hanging Gardens were cultivated using hydroponic methods. Philo believed that the plants were grown in containers rather than in the ground. He also states that the upper terrace of the gardens was embedded with the roots of the plants, providing a sophisticated agricultural system for its time. The gardens were supported by stone columns and had streams of water that came from elevated sources that flowed through sloped channels, helping to water the entire garden and maintain the plants' moisture levels and overall greenery. The gardens were truly a masterpiece and a fitting tribute to the king who commissioned them.

Flavius Josephus, a Roman historian who lived in the 1st century CE and was familiar with the work of Berossus, a Babylonian priest, offered a different perspective on the Hanging Gardens. In his book *Against Apion,* Josephus stated that King Nebuchadnezzar II built the gardens to make his queen happy, as she was originally from Media and enjoyed being in an area that featured hills. However, this account is only a passing reference, and there is little concrete evidence to support it. Some older works suggest that a Syrian ruler was responsible for building the Hanging Gardens, but again, there is little information regarding the specifics of this construction.

It is worth noting that the exact location and even the identity of the ruler who commissioned the gardens remains a mystery and is still debated among scholars. The accounts of early historians are not consistent and may contain errors or exaggerations. The gardens' water supply and irrigation system are not well understood, and there is debate over how they were able to maintain the plants.

Regardless, the most popular theory remains that the Hanging Gardens were built by King Nebuchadnezzar II to please his wife, Amytis. Irrigation systems, using bitumen, reeds, and lead, were likely used to collect water from the Euphrates and disperse it into the air to support the gardens. The Archimedes screw could have potentially been used, as it lifts materials (in this case, water) from a low point to a high point. However, the Archimedes screw was not invented until around 250 BCE, which means the Babylonians would have come up with their own version and neglected to write it down or use it elsewhere.

The Controversies Surrounding the Hanging Gardens

As you can imagine, historians and archaeologists have long disputed the Hanging Gardens of Babylon. People commonly assume the gardens existed in Babylon during Nebuchadnezzar II's reign, but there is little to no evidence to support this. In fact, there is no mention of the Hanging Gardens in any of the Babylonian literature. Nothing has yet been unearthed during archaeological digs that can be utilized to confirm the existence of the gardens.

During Nebuchadnezzar's reign, stone tablets meticulously describe Babylon, including the palace and its diverse military fortifications. So, it seems odd that there is no mention of the Hanging Gardens. This scarcity of concrete evidence has led some scholars to believe the Hanging Gardens is nothing but a myth.

There are three predominant hypotheses about the Hanging Gardens of Babylon. Firstly, they might have existed solely as an elaborate legend. Within the works of Strabo, Diodorus, Siculus, and Quintus Curtius Rufus, a more romanticized portrayal emerges, with these exquisite gardens bestowing verdancy and awe upon the city of Babylon. The second theory proposes that the Hanging Gardens could have once flourished in Babylon, only to meet their demise during the 1st century CE. Alternatively, these gardens might have originally belonged to Assyrian King Sennacherib. We already explored the notion that the Hanging Gardens could have been constructed in the city of Nineveh, situated on the Tigris River near modern-day Mosul in Iraq. That is a possibility, but it is also possible that Sennacherib, who ruled from 704 to 681 BCE, built a magnificent garden in Nineveh that became conflated with the legendary Hanging Gardens.

The term "Babylon" itself was frequently employed to denote the entire region of Mesopotamia. This usage likely contributed to the confusion surrounding the precise location of the Hanging Gardens. The Greek historians who chronicled the gardens might have been alluding to the general vicinity rather than a specific city when using the name Babylon.

Stephanie Dalley, a British Assyriologist and scholar, argues that the Hanging Gardens of Babylon is the garden mentioned by Assyrian King Sennacherib in his inscriptions. Dalley believes that, over time, the location has been misunderstood and attributed to Babylon, which is a more memorable capital. She also points to the archaeological discoveries of enormous aqueduct networks in the region of Nineveh, as well as inscriptions that point to Sennacherib's garden. The area consists of a network of canals, dams, and aqueducts that span fifty miles and was used to transport water to Nineveh. It also contains water-raising screws that were used to transport water to the upper levels of the gardens.

Assyriologist Laurie Pearce proposed that the Hanging Gardens might have been a military garden, possibly established in the space left by the destruction of Nineveh in 612 BCE. She also suggested that there might have been a variety of herbs and plants growing in the gardens, including garlic, coriander, fenugreek, dill, and a range of tree species, including cedars. However, due to the lack of concrete information, it is impossible to determine the precise types of plants that grew in the gardens, if they even existed at all.

Despite the lack of archaeological evidence for the existence of the Hanging Gardens of Babylon, it is possible that evidence of their existence is buried deep within the Euphrates River and cannot be securely recovered. The flow of the Euphrates River has changed throughout the millennia, so it is possible that any signs of the gardens' existence have been buried beneath the waters of the river.

Additionally, it has been hypothesized that Nebuchadnezzar's name may have been given to the gardens for political reasons and that the actual site of the gardens may have been located elsewhere.

The mystery of the Hanging Gardens may never be fully solved.

An Assyrian wall relief depicting the gardens in Nineveh.
https://commons.wikimedia.org/wiki/File:Gardens_of_Ninevah.png

Historians have also considered the possibility that Alexander the Great's troops, who were known to be impressed by the vast affluence of the thriving metropolis of Babylon, might have exaggerated their experiences and memories of the city upon returning to their homeland. This could have led to the embellishment of stories about the grand gardens, palm trees, and towering buildings of Mesopotamia.

To sum up, the existence of the Hanging Gardens remains a topic of debate among scholars. While some argue that the gardens were a myth or were located in another city, others propose that the gardens existed in Babylon but have yet to be discovered. Further research and archaeological discoveries are necessary to uncover the truth about the Hanging Gardens of Babylon.

Gardens in the Ancient World

The ancient world witnessed the birth of gardens, which originated in the Fertile Crescent, transcending their purpose from mere sustenance to sources of pleasure. This novel concept swiftly disseminated across the sprawling landscapes of the Mediterranean and Mesopotamia, gradually becoming a hallmark of opulence for the affluent. Architects embellished gardens with splendid sculptures, captivating water features, and architectural marvels.

A fascinating trend emerged as artisans adept in the art of fresco techniques began to seamlessly integrate the imagery of gardens into their masterpieces. Vibrant depictions adorned villa walls, conjuring the illusion of stepping into a verdant sanctuary upon entering a room. Notable examples of this artistic fusion can be found in the exquisite frescoes discovered in the ancient city of Pompeii.

The Hanging Gardens of Babylon were not the only gardens to appear in ancient Mesopotamia. One other notable example is the gardens at Pasargadae. Constructed by Cyrus the Great in the Zagros Mountains around 550 BCE, these gardens featured terraces for irrigation, tall walls for shade, and trees grouped together to retain moisture and withstand the harsh winds. The gardens were located near an abundant water supply. The connection between gardens and palaces can also be observed in other ancient cultures, such as China and Mesoamerica, which makes it plausible that the gardens of Pasargadae were located close to a palace. It is impossible for us to know what the Hanging Gardens of Babylon looked like (unless we trust the ancient Greeks and Romans), so examining what other ancient gardens looked like gives us a better idea of what the Hanging Gardens might have looked like.

After Nebuchadnezzar's reign, Babylon continued to develop as a great city under the authority of the Achaemenid Empire (550–330 BCE) and Seleucid Empire (312–63 BCE). It is stated that both empires made frequent use of the palaces in Babylon as their residential palaces. There is a very good chance that the gardens were still in existence many centuries after the structure was completed, as the city was reported to have kept its strategic significance for many years.

In 1899 CE, archaeological investigations in Babylon began to take on a more methodical approach. However, there have been no significant findings of the Hanging Gardens. Nevertheless, other ancient monuments, like the double walls and the Ishtar Gate, were found during excavations. During one excavation, fourteen vaulted rooms belonging to the South Palace of Babylon were uncovered. It is possible that more information on the gardens might be unearthed the more excavations are made.

For instance, excavations were carried out close to the river that gave the impression of the site being the king's palace. These excavations uncovered walls, drains, and something that could be a reservoir, all of which are typical structures for gardens; however, there was no evidence to prove that this location was the Hanging Gardens.

It is difficult to believe that the gardens never existed because their story is so widespread. It is hard to imagine that an ancient scholar came up the Hanging Gardens on a whim, although the possibility cannot be ruled out. If the writer was being meticulous about their work, they would have based their information on something, and it is possible that that "something" has disappeared. Additionally, the Hanging Gardens have been on the list of the Seven Wonders of the Ancient World for a long time. It is also entirely possible that the Hanging Gardens of Babylon should have been called the Hanging Gardens of Nineveh.

Summary of Events

- 605 BCE–562 BCE: King Nebuchadnezzar II reigns as king of Babylon and is credited with constructing the Hanging Gardens of Babylon, at least according to tradition.

- c. 575 BCE: Nebuchadnezzar II constructs the Ishtar Gate and the massive walls of Babylon.

- 225 BCE: The Seven Wonders of the Ancient World is formalized by Philo of Byzantium. The list included the Hanging Gardens of Babylon.

- 1st century CE: If the Hanging Gardens existed, it has been theorized they were destroyed in the 1st century CE. However, they could have fallen into disrepair centuries before.

Chapter 3 – Temple of Artemis

According to Greek mythology, Artemis was said to have ruled over the flora and fauna, fertility, and other natural forces. She was also the goddess of chastity and hunting. The most notable temple dedicated to Artemis, which was known as Artemesium, was located in Ephesus (modern-day Turkey). The temple was rebuilt more than once, with the first temple being built sometime in the 8th century BCE. The current theory is that this temple was wiped out by a flood since the region is prone to flooding. The second, more iconic structure took around 120 years to build.[3]

Construction of the second temple began during the rule of a Lydian king named Croesus (r. 560–546 BCE). King Croesus took over Ephesus sometime between 560 and 550 BCE. After his victory, he started building the Temple of Artemis.

The Roman historian Pliny the Elder, who lived in the 1st century CE, stated that Chersiphron of Knossos built the second reconstruction of the Temple of Artemis, which measured more than 370 feet by 150 feet. However, Strabo believed that Chersiphron had help from his son, Metagenes. Strabo's theory seems more probable, as constructing a temple of this size would have been a massive undertaking. The Ephesians even believed that Artemis built the temple since the temple's blocks above the columns weighed twenty-four tons each.

---

[3] This number comes from Pliny the Elder, a Roman historian, so it is possible the temple did not take this long to build.

Pliny states that when the work site was damp, charcoal seams and sheepskins were layered upon one another. The temple was also reconstructed on the same site as the original since it was believed the location would protect it from earthquakes. It is thought to be one of the largest Greek temples to ever be constructed. It was even bigger than the Parthenon!

According to Pliny the Elder, the temple consisted of 127 columns, each approximately 60 feet in height. Vitruvius, a Roman architect from the 1ˢᵗ century BCE, described the temple as dipteral octastyle, meaning it had two rows of columns around the temple with eight columns on each of the front and back façades. The Ionic columns were said to have Greek mythical figures inscribed on them, and Amazons were painted on the shrine's ornamental mural.

According to Pliny the Elder, the second temple took around 120 years to construct, lasting from 550 to 430 BCE. There are various accounts of the temple's destruction, with one story stating that it was burned down by Herostratus in an attempt to make his name famous. Apparently, Herostratus was sentenced to death because of his actions. People also could no longer speak his name since the authorities did not want his name to be remembered; of course, someone jotted it down as we know his name today.

Herostratus allegedly did this on Alexander the Great's birthday (July 21ˢᵗ, 356 BCE). Another account, this one by Plutarch (born in the 1ˢᵗ century CE), relates to Alexander the Great's birth. According to legend, Artemis was assisting in the delivery of Alexander the Great on that day and was not present at the temple.

According to tradition, in 333 BCE, Alexander the Great visited Ephesus and expressed a desire to sponsor the temple's reconstruction as long as his name was placed on it. However, the leaders were hesitant to engrave his name on the temple. They respectfully declined, saying that it would be inappropriate for the name of one deity to appear beside that of another.

Nevertheless, in 323 BCE, the temple was rebuilt, with Macedonian architect Dinocrates playing a role in the reconstruction. He worked diligently to restore every aspect of the once-majestic structure. The temple housed an array of artistic treasures, including a captivating portrait of Alexander the Great painted by the celebrated artist Apelles.

The temple served as a hub for pilgrims for centuries. However, the Ostrogoths attacked the city in 262 CE. They sacked the temple. Some sources say it was not rebuilt, so the temple must not have been completely razed since people still used it. However, it would never reach its former glory again. In 380 CE, Christianity was acknowledged as the official state religion of the Roman Empire (of which Ephesus was part), and about ten years later, Emperor Theodosius outlawed paganism and declared all pagan temples should be shut down. It is believed that the temple was destroyed by Christian believers in 401 CE. It would not be rebuilt again.

There are various accounts of the Artemesium's destruction. According to the Acts of John (a collection of stories about the Apostle John), John issued a death threat to the general populace and prayed to God for forgiveness on account of the people's foolishness. As a result, the altar of the Temple of Artemis fractured into a great number of pieces. The statues of more than seven gods were shattered into a thousand pieces, and the temple's ceiling collapsed, resulting in the death of a priest.

There are also reports from the Syriac *History of John*, which indicates that the priests recanted their beliefs and beat their faces with grief. They walked away from the altar, went to John, and prostrated themselves in front of him. After that, they wrapped ropes around the statue of Artemis and toppled it. However, the most likely explanation is that Christians tore down the temple, which was likely already lying in ruins, in the early 5th century CE.

The Temple of Artemis was included on the list of the Seven Wonders of the Ancient World after it was built for the second time. This is what the site looks like today.
FDV, CC BY-SA 4.0 <https://creativecommons.org/licenses/by-sa/4.0>, via Wikimedia Commons; https://commons.wikimedia.org/wiki/File:Templo-Artemisa-Efeso-2017.jpg

Who Is Artemis?

Artemis, also known as Diana in Roman mythology, holds a significant place in Greek lore as the twin sister of Apollo. Revered as the patroness of hunters and wild animals, she is often depicted with her iconic bow and arrow. Artemis, one of the revered twelve Olympian deities in Greek mythology, presided over an array of domains, including nature, the moon, chastity, hunting, and childbirth.

As the daughter of Leto and Zeus and the twin sister of Apollo, Artemis fiercely protected her virginity and the purity of her priestesses. Iconic portrayals often depicted her as a youthful huntress astride a stag or another majestic creature, brandishing her bow. Despite her role as a guardian of women and young girls, Artemis was not associated with procreation, and her narratives frequently emphasized the importance of chastity.

Throughout Greece, shrines and temples devoted to Artemis were scattered far and wide, with renowned sanctuaries gracing locations like Brauron and Karyai. Artemis's stories, such as transforming her hunting companion Callisto into a bear or her plea to Asclepius to resurrect Hippolytus after he pledged to lead a celibate life, further underscored her fervent dedication to safeguarding the purity of her priestesses and her detachment from fertility worship.

Interestingly, the first Temple of Artemis, constructed by the Ionians, was believed to be situated in Ortygia, near Ephesus, rather than on the renowned island of Delos. This temple, dating back to the 8th century BCE, unfortunately met its demise due to a devastating flood in the 7th century BCE. Recent archaeological discoveries have shed light on this catastrophe, yet the fate of the original temples remains shrouded in mystery.

According to legend, the statue of the goddess Artemis, which held a special place of worship within the temple, was discovered by Amazons hailing from northern Turkey. However, additional details are required to validate the accuracy of this tale and to unravel the circumstances surrounding the construction of the initial temple. The remaining sculptures of Artemis in Ephesus portray her standing with her knees together and arms outstretched in front of her, elegantly adorned in a long skirt adorned with animal motifs.

It is believed that Artemis of Ephesus was influenced by other deities, such as Isis and Cybele, showcasing the profound impact of local beliefs and customs on the development of Greek religion. Beyond her role as the goddess of fertility, Artemis held the esteemed position of the city's guardian. As the temple's popularity grew, an influx of tourists and devout followers of Artemis brought lavish offerings of jewelry and financial contributions, significantly bolstering the city's coffers. Ephesus eventually became renowned as a sanctuary for individuals seeking refuge from persecution. Even the Amazons supposedly made two separate journeys to the city in search of solace.

Where Was the Temple of Artemis Located?

The convergence of Greek and local cultures is exemplified in the ancient city of Ephesus, located near the modern Turkish city of Selçuk. This region has been inhabited by humans for millennia, but the city's prominence rose during the early Bronze Age. However, it was not until the 11th or 10th century BCE that the city was called Ephesus. Despite this, the local inhabitants continued to exert significant influence. A prime example of this cultural blending is the unification of the Greek goddess Artemis and the regional fertility goddess Cybele. Scholars believe the site of the Temple of Artemis was a sacred place devoted to the veneration of the mother goddess since the Bronze Age.

The Ionians established the ancient city of Ephesus in the 11th or 10th century BCE. It was located at the base of Ayasuluk Hill in present-day Turkey and served as a prominent trade hub in the eastern Mediterranean.

Throughout the majority of its existence, Ephesus was a port city. Its decline was due to wars and ecological difficulties. The city was situated on the Aegean Sea at the mouth of the Kaystros River, which emptied into a bay. However, sediment slowly filled the river, obstructing harbor access. Because of sediment buildup, Ephesus was relocated five times. As time went on, the region around the city became sandier, and it is now receding from the ocean.

The location of the renowned Temple of Artemis faced issues of frequent flooding and marshy conditions as early as the 8th century. A previous worship center dedicated to Artemis was destroyed by devastating floods.

Relics of the Temple of Artemis

The revered Temple of Artemis showcased magnificent statues skillfully crafted by artists, although the original bronze masterpieces have regrettably been lost to the ravages of time. Nevertheless, reproductions created during the Roman era offer a glimpse into the appearance of these statues. They portrayed a majestic female figure of similar height, stature, and attire, often with her right arm gracefully raised above her head or occasionally resting on a spear.

The artifacts mentioned in this section primarily pertain to the later Temple of Artemis (the one on the list of the Seven Wonders of the Ancient World), which began construction sometime around 323 BC. The earlier two builds of the temple have limited surviving evidence.

The Lady of Ephesus.
Gargarapalvin, CC BY-SA 4.0 <https://creativecommons.org/licenses/by-sa/4.0>, via Wikimedia Commons; https://commons.wikimedia.org/wiki/File:Efes_M%C3%BCzesi,_2019_11.jpg

Within the esteemed halls of the National Archaeological Museum of Naples, one can encounter an Ephesian worship statue that dates back to the 2nd century CE. This particular statue deviates from the commonly associated Roman representation of Diana, showcasing the deity adorned with a modius (a headdress), meticulously crafted from alabaster and bronze and positioned atop her head. Furthermore, the statue incorporates depictions of breasts, eggs, or perhaps the testicles of sacrificial bulls, symbolizing ideas of fertility and abundance. Another modius from the later temple is currently on display at the Museo del Palazzo dei Conservatori in Rome.

The pediment, the triangular gable adorning the front of the later temple, is believed to have featured three windows or apertures, likely depicting intricately adorned scenes. It is speculated that one of the bronze statues depicting the Amazons might have been positioned in this area. However, only fragments of the pediment have withstood the test of time, leaving the full image of the Temple of Artemis shrouded in mystery.

A model of the third Temple of Artemis located in Istanbul, Turkey

The later Temple of Artemis, which was extensively explored and excavated by John Turtle Wood with the invaluable support of the British Museum during the late 19th century, has yielded remarkable discoveries, including the temple's foundation and an immense column drum. Wood's six-year quest culminated in the unearthing of the temple's buried pavement in 1869. Situated approximately twenty feet below the marshy terrain, the excavation of the pavement necessitated the acquisition of the entire property to ensure cost-effectiveness. Extracting the pavement alone would have entailed significant expenses.

During the meticulous excavation process, an enormous column drum weighing over eleven tons was discovered in September 1871. The drum was partially submerged in water and inverted. Wood employed his expertise to restore the column drum to its original position by constructing supporting columns and elevating it. After two arduous months of work, the marble drum was cautiously wrapped and prepared for transportation to the British Museum. Twenty dray horses were used to transport it!

Upon closer scrutiny of the six feet by six feet marble drum, scholars noticed intricate carvings of a woman, potentially representing Alcestis or Eurydice. The figure of Hermes Psychopompus, renowned for guiding spirits to the underworld, was sculpted. He holds a caduceus. The left side of the drum showcased Thanatos, the personification of death, while Persephone and Pluto (or Hades in Greek mythology), the rulers of the underworld, were depicted on the right side. If authenticated as the work of Scopas, one of the illustrious sculptors of that era, this discovery would hold significant artistic and historical significance. Nevertheless, uncertainties persist about the temple, such as whether the structure had an outdoor area or was covered with wooden tiles.

Archaic Temple Adornments.

The embellishments of the older temples are a subject of fascination. It is said that the second temple was an intricate structure with a rooftop that provided shelter to the altar. Recent archaeological discoveries provide evidence of the earlier temples' existence, although information on what the first temple would have looked like is scarce.

The second temple was believed to have been built between the 6th and 4th centuries BCE. The ornate decorations of the temple, consisting of friezes and other embellishments, were located on the lower drums of the columns, the parapets, and the columns themselves. These adornments would have been popular during the Ionic era. Depictions of various animals and horses on some of the pieces of the frieze have been, indicating some sort of procession.

Historians know this version of the temple was important, as more than one thousand objects were left behind at the site dating to this period, including some of the earliest coins in history. Records indicate that it was around 377 feet (115 meters) long and a little over 150 feet

(46 meters) wide. It was supposedly built of marble, which would have made it the first Greek temple made out of that material.

The second temple had a double row of columns that formed a passage around the inner chamber, which would have held an image of Artemis. According to Pliny the Elder, these columns were forty feet (thirteen meters) high and intricately carved.

The Altar

The Temple of Artemis in Ephesus is a fitting location for the grand altar, which measures 39.70 meters in length and 16.67 meters in width. It was shaped like a horseshoe. The Ephesus Archaeological Research Institute unearthed several polygonal or trapezoidal slabs from the ancient temple's soil, which contain remnants of walls on the south, east, and north sides. The Hellenistic temple had a base with 3.4 meters on each side that faced west and was adorned with two rows of columns instead of walls. The priests could ascend the altar via a ramp, thanks to its horseshoe design and elevated position.

The altar was not solely a place of worship but also a separate structure that was part of the larger temple. Given the considerable number of merchants, service providers, refugees, and asylum seekers who visited the site, it is not surprising that the altar stood out from the rest of the temple.

Hellenistic Temple Description

The architectural layout of the third reconstruction of the Temple of Artemis appears to be quite standard, consisting of a stairway running up from the basement to the main building. The main building is believed to have measured around 344 feet (105 meters) in length and around 180 feet (55 meters) in width and features two rows of columns that are almost 60 feet (17.6 meters) in height. The sculptures and bas-reliefs that decorated this temple were similar to those seen in other ancient temples.

The actual structure of the building had a rectangular outline. However, the exterior of the walls did not take the form of a giant rectangle but rather two smaller sides that were set at a lower level. This resulted in the formation of a naos, or sanctuary, on the side of the entrance and a posticum, or back room, on the side facing away from the entrance.

Despite having a rectangular shape, the hall was broken up into three distinct portions. A roof that was supported by four columns could be found above the vestibule, which was found just behind the entrance. The temple's treasury could be found on the left side of the building, while the steps were found on the right. The cella, also known as the main room (the room where the image of the goddess was placed), was situated in the middle of the building.

What Happened to the Temple?

As mentioned, the first version of the temple was likely destroyed in a flood. The second version was burned down by Herostratus. Some believe that he might not have set fire to the temple, though. To truly destroy the temple via burning, he would have had to set fire to the wooden roof. Doubters of him being the culprit find it unlikely that no one stopped him, especially considering the temple was well guarded. Another theory is that the temple administrators purposefully set the temple on fire since it was sinking and needed to be rebuilt.

The third temple became disused as time passed. Christianity rose in popularity, with the traditional Greek and Roman religions being abandoned. In 262, the Goths sacked the temple. Since Artemis was no longer worshiped as much as she had in the past, it is likely the temple sat in its derelict state until Christianity became the official religion of the Roman Empire. It is possible that a Christian mob destroyed whatever was still standing of the building in 401 CE.

Some of the stones of the Temple of Artemis were used to construct other buildings, but it is not known for sure what buildings were built on the foundation of one of the Seven Wonders of the Ancient World. Some say the Hagia Sophia contains stones from the temple, but this seems highly unlikely.

The Impact of the Temple of Artemis

The Temple of Artemis transcended its role as a mere site of worship. Historical records attest to the temple serving as a bank. Its strategic positioning permitted it to be somewhat removed from the machinations going on in Ephesus, which allowed it to stay dedicated to the reasons it was created in the first place. The Temple of Artemis in Ephesus was also used for a very long time, considering it was built in the Bronze Age and still had worshipers visit during the Roman Empire. The veneration of Artemis of Ephesus proliferated across the Aegean Sea, Anatolia, the Mediterranean Basin, and even the Iberian Peninsula.

The portrayal of Artemis of Ephesus was unparalleled in comparison to other representations of the goddess. The esteemed custodian of the temple, known as the *megabyse*, wielded authority on par with the magistrates of Ephesus during the peak of the temple's influence. The Temple of Artemis also acquired a reputation that forbade any desecration or intrusion by other factions, including the Lydians, Athenians, Persians, and Spartans. Not even the formidable Alexander the Great could assert dominion over the sacred grounds.

Summary of Events

- 7th century BCE – The first Temple of Artemis was destroyed, likely by a flood.
- c. 550 BCE – The reconstruction of the Temple of Artemis began in Ephesus.
- 356 BCE – The Temple of Artemis was destroyed by a fire.
- 323 BCE – The Temple of Artemis was rebuilt yet again.
- 2nd century BCE – Antipater of Sidon includes the Temple of Artemis on his list of the Seven Wonders of the Ancient World.
- 262 CE – The Temple of Artemis was plundered by the Goths.
- 401 CE – The Temple of Artemis was possibly destroyed by a Christian mob. If this did not occur, then the temple was destroyed in some other way.

Chapter 4 – The Statue of Zeus

The Statue of Zeus stood in the ancient world for almost one thousand years in the sanctuary of Olympia, located in the Peloponnese Peninsula. It is believed that the statue oversaw the ancient Olympic Games. The first Olympic Games are believed to have been held in 776 BCE and were considered a significant event in the history of Greece, with the date of the games and the name of the first foot-race winner, Coroebus of Elis (who was a cook), being widely known among the Greek population.

Who Was Zeus?

Zeus, known as Jupiter in Roman mythology, was the supreme deity in Greek and Roman mythology. His multifaceted nature and the diverse roles he played made him a figure of great importance.

Firstly, Zeus was regarded as the god presiding over the air. He possessed the power to unleash storms and tempests. This portrayal emphasized his dominion over the forces of nature, showcasing his ability to command the elements and inspire awe in the hearts of mortals.

Secondly, Zeus personified the laws of nature and embodied the unchanging and harmonious order that governed the physical and moral realms. As a deity associated with the laws of the universe, he represented the immutable principles that regulated the natural world and the conduct of individuals. His influence extended beyond the mere physical realm and encompassed the moral fabric of society.

Furthermore, Zeus was revered as the guardian of state life and the progenitor of kingly power. He played a crucial role in the establishment and preservation of political institutions, symbolizing the fundamental authority that underpinned the governance of states and the rule of kings. The Greeks looked upon Zeus as their protector, recognizing his importance in maintaining stability and order within their communities.

Lastly, Zeus held the esteemed position of being the father of gods and men. As the divine patriarch, he assumed the responsibility of overseeing the actions and well-being of both deities and mortals. His paternal role signified his concern for the welfare of all beings and highlighted his involvement in the affairs of the celestial and earthly realms.

Greek mythology is replete with numerous myths and stories surrounding Zeus, each contributing to the intricate tapestry of his character. One particularly well-known myth revolves around Zeus's upbringing. According to the tale, Zeus was concealed by his mother, Rhea, to safeguard him from his father, Cronus, who harbored fears that one of his offspring would overthrow him. Raised in secrecy on the island of Crete, Zeus eventually returned to dethrone Cronus and ascended as the ruler of the gods.

Another popular myth involving Zeus is the narrative of the flood. Disillusioned by the corruption and wickedness among humanity, Zeus decided to send a deluge to wipe out all the mortals. Yet, he spared Deucalion and Pyrrha, a righteous couple, who were instructed to repopulate the earth by casting stones over their shoulders, which miraculously transformed into human beings.

These stories serve as a testament to Zeus's immense power, authority, and active participation in the affairs of gods and humans. They exemplify his capacity to influence the course of events, showcase his role as a moral arbiter, and underscore his commitment to the dispensation of justice. Overall, Zeus was venerated and worshiped by the Greeks for his dominion over the natural world, his guidance in matters of state, and his paternal concern for the well-being of mortals.

The Temple of Olympia: Pre-Statue of Zeus

Olympia, nestled in the enchanting region of Elis within the sprawling western Peloponnese Peninsula, welcomed weary souls embroiled in the labyrinthine web of Greek factions locked in perpetual conflict. Seeking solace and security, people flocked to this idyllic haven. And in Olympia, an unparalleled spectacle unfolded—the inaugural Olympic Games, which became an ode to human prowess and camaraderie.

A stadium served as the stage for these momentous games and their accompanying festivities, while the Altis, a sanctuary within the city, flourished with magnificent temples.

In 590 BCE, a temple honoring the sacred bond between Hera and Zeus was built. Hera, the goddess of femininity and childbirth, was the wife of Zeus, the mighty deity presiding over lightning, thunder, and life-giving rain. These divine figures, the quintessential king and queen of all Hellenic gods, were celebrated at the Temple of Hera, the oldest temple in Olympia. Their sculpted forms were enshrined within the sanctified walls of the temple. Hera was seated regally beside Zeus, who stood as her steadfast guardian. Once the Temple of Zeus was built, he was no longer worshiped as much at this temple, allowing Hera to become the predominant one.

Within the sacred confines of this celestial sanctuary, ancient flames danced upon the altars of old. Today, the Olympic flame is lit within its ruins, still illuminating the past and present. The temple was destroyed sometime in the early 4th century CE due to an earthquake.

Sometime in the 5th century BCE, a little over a century after the inception of the Temple of Hera, the seeds of a new temple were sown. A symphony of artistry and craftsmanship sprouted, birthing the Temple of Zeus, a monument that would command reverence and admiration for generations to come. This architectural masterpiece finished construction in 456 BCE. It stood tall, an epitome of beauty and wonder.

Inside the temple, a colossal statue of Zeus reigned supreme, its sheer magnitude dwarfing mortal comprehension. Honored as one of the Seven Wonders of the Ancient World, this divine effigy imbued the sanctum with an awe-inspiring aura.

Thus, Olympia remains etched in the annals of history, not only because of the famed Olympic Games but also because of the people's reverence and architectural creations.

The Temple of Zeus

In the 5th century BCE, Olympia experienced much prosperity, as it was a time when grandeur and ambition melded seamlessly. It was during this era that the construction of a colossal Doric temple with a six-by-thirteen column layout commenced. The Eleans, enriched by their triumph against the Triphylians, generously financed this monumental undertaking. A mastermind by the name of Libon of Elis shepherded the project to completion in 456 BCE. Libon's crowning achievement, the Temple of Zeus, is renowned far and wide and is believed to have provided inspiration for the illustrious Parthenon that would grace the Athenian landscape in later years.

The Temple of Zeus, an imposing rectangular edifice oriented from east to west, boasted an array of sculptures and other embellishments that dazzled the people who visited it. Accounts relayed by Pausanias, a distinguished Greek geographer and writer of the 2nd century CE, describe a towering structure reaching a lofty height of 68 feet (21 meters) and stretching 95 feet (29 meters) wide and 230 feet (70 meters) in length. This magnificent temple proudly displayed thirteen columns on its elongated sides and six columns on its shorter sides. Crafted from local limestone and adorned with a white plaster coating, these columns provided support for the resplendent white marble roof.

The temple's interior embraced a minimalist aesthetic, a canvas of simplicity designed to elevate the awe-inspiring centerpiece—the Statue of Zeus. Built around 435 BCE, this sculpture commanded attention, casting a spell of reverence upon all who set foot within the temple. While the interior exuded restraint, the exterior walls depicted tales of Greek mythology on the pediments, the triangular spaces above the doorway. The eastern pediment narrated the thrilling chariot scene from the tale of Pelops and Oenomaus, while the western pediment immortalized the legendary clash between the Lapiths and the Centaurs. Some of these remarkable pieces of art still exist today, serving as enchanting relics and guardians of timeless legends begging to be retold.

To truly unravel the intricate tale of Oenomaus and Pelops, one must first explore the narrative of Tantalus, Pelops's ill-fated father. Born of Zeus and the nymph Pluto's divine union, Tantalus wielded immense power and basked in the gods' favor as the ruler of Phrygia. However, his hubris and insolence led him astray, as he dared to betray the deities by serving his own son in a feast to the immortal beings as a way to test their powers.

Swift retribution descended upon Tantalus, with the gods banishing him to the depths of Hades, consigning him to eternal torment for his transgressions. However, a glimmer of mercy shone through Zeus, as he was moved by compassion for the tragic Pelops. One of the Fates resurrected the young prince, although he was missing a piece of his body, his shoulder, which had been eaten by one of the gods. An ivory prosthetic replaced the missing shoulder. Pelops fled to the sanctuary of Pisa after being unseated by King Ilus of Troy, setting the stage for a fateful encounter.

Within the realm of Pisa, Pelops found himself entangled in the destiny-shaping web of King Oenomaus, the proud father of the captivating maiden, Hippodamia. The king devised a treacherous chariot race, a daring test of skill and courage, with the hand of Hippodamia as the coveted prize. Thirteen suitors had already met their tragic end trying to win her hand.

Unfazed by the inherent danger, Pelops embraced the race with unyielding confidence, a conviction borne from his divine equine companions and the benevolence of the gods. Guided by the clandestine aid of Hermes and the king's own charioteer, Myrtilus, who covertly tampered with Oenomaus's chariot, Pelops emerged triumphant. The king's ill-fated vehicle careened off course, sealing his own tragic fate.

As the conqueror of the race, Pelops claimed Hippodamia as his beloved bride. In gratitude for Myrtilus's assistance, Pelops rewarded the charioteer. Yet, consumed by insatiable greed, Myrtilus yearned for more, conspiring to orchestrate Pelops's downfall. Their tumultuous conflict reached its climax with the fateful demise of Myrtilus, who cursed Pelops and his progeny.

This curse cast a long, ominous shadow over the House of Atreus, culminating in the tragic saga of Agamemnon and Clytemnestra. Nevertheless, Pelops succeeded in establishing a powerful dynasty in Pisa, forever intertwining his name with the origins of the illustrious Olympic Games.

As one wandered through the hallowed halls of the Temple of Zeus, one couldn't help but be transfixed by the pivotal moments of Pelops's extraordinary journey. Today, the temple's intricate sculptures, including metopes, which fill the space between triglyphs (the ends of the wooden beams holding the roof), portraying the legendary Hercules undertaking his mighty labors, can be admired at the Olympia Museum.

An illustration of what the Temple of Zeus might have looked like. This illustration was made in the early 20ᵗʰ century.

Master Sculptor Phidias

In the vast and ancient realm of Greece, where history intertwines with myth and legends, Olympia stood as a jewel cherished by the polis of Elis. Its magnetic allure drew in visitors from near and far, from wide-eyed tourists seeking adventure to devout pilgrims in search of spiritual solace. Olympia also attracted sports enthusiasts who traveled from all corners of the Mediterranean to witness the exhilarating competitive games held there.

Olympia sought to become a place where gods and mortals converged, a nexus of divine energy that would leave a mark on the annals of history. At the heart of this endeavor stood Zeus, the supreme ruler of the Olympian gods, a towering figure whose influence permeated every aspect of the religious and cultural fabric of ancient Greece.

To honor and appease the mighty Zeus, a monument of his glory was deemed necessary—an offering that would encapsulate the collective devotion and awe of the Greek people. So, the esteemed Phidias, a visionary among mortals, was bestowed with the responsibility of bringing this ambitious vision to life. With unparalleled craftsmanship and boundless creativity, Phidias embarked on a journey that would alter the course of Olympia's destiny.

In the 20th century CE, a flurry of excavations took place; it was as if the earth itself yearned to reveal the secrets buried within its bosom. During this meticulous unraveling of time's tapestry, an astonishing discovery emerged—an intricate workshop, a testament to Phidias's tireless labor. Within the fragmented remnants of the workshop, several treasures of the past, such as tools and materials, emerged. Most noticeably, archaeologists found a red-figure Attic cup delicately adorned with the words *Pheidio eimi* ("I belong to Phidias"); however, many historians believe the inscription to be a forgery.

Phidias's creative genius was not a solitary endeavor; it took a team of skilled craftsmen and artisans, each contributing their unique talents. As Phidias carefully set his plans in motion, the temple's interior became a sanctuary for artists. With meticulous precision, the ivory and gold plates were shaped and polished, melding together to form the statue's lifelike skin. Zeus wore a crown of olive leaves and donned a robe made of glass. According to Pausanias, who detailed the sculpture in vivid detail, the robe was covered with lilies and animals. The king of the Olympians held a statue of Nike, the goddess of victory, in one hand, and in the other was a scepter. The statue, a majestic, seated figure towering at an impressive twelve meters, was meticulously fashioned by Phidias using a striking combination of ivory and gold.

Of course, a king needs a throne. The Statue of Zeus, which measured around forty feet (twelve meters) tall, sat on an immaculate throne decorated with gold, ivory, and other precious materials. Panaenus, Phidias's brother, is thought to have been the one who painted the throne. The floor in front of the statue was paved with black tiles, and there was a pool of oil, which was used to help keep the ivory in pristine condition.

According to legend, Phidias was so overcome once he finished that he prayed to Zeus, asking if his work was good enough. A lightning bolt struck the floor, signifying Zeus's delight with the sculpture. Those who saw the statue say that it was one of the most awe-inspiring things they had witnessed. For instance, Livy said the Roman general Aemilius Paullus is said to have been "moved to his soul, as if he had seen the god in person."

Alas, even the mightiest of mortals can succumb to the fickle winds of fate. Phidias went on to create another amazing work of art, the *Athena Parthenos*, in the Parthenon. However, once the work was completed,

Phidias was accused of stealing money. It is likely the charges were false, as he was very close with Pericles, the ruler of Athens. Pericles had many enemies, so it is very plausible that the charges were made up to get back at Pericles.

Phidias supposedly tried to prove his innocence by showing that the gold he had stolen was actually used in the *Athena Parthenos*. But another charge appeared in its place. He had placed his image and that of Pericles on Athena's shield, which would have been viewed as blasphemy. This charge was likely to be true. Phidias was placed in prison, where he died.

Though the Statue of Zeus itself has been lost to the unforgiving currents of time, it is still remembered in history as one of the Seven Wonders of the Ancient World. Fragments of the grand Temple of Zeus still stand, weathered by time, while remnants of Phidias's workshop provide a glimpse into the inner workings of a mastermind.

The legacy of Phidias lives on, not just in the remnants of Olympia but also in the countless replicas that dot the Mediterranean landscape.

The most accurate reproduction of the Athena Parthenos.
Photo by George E. Koronaios, cropped by Neoclassicism Enthusiast, CC BY-SA 4.0
<https://creativecommons.org/licenses/by-sa/4.0>, via Wikimedia Commons;
https://commons.wikimedia.org/wiki/File:Statuette_of_Athena_(3rd_cent._A.D.)_in_the_National_Archaeological_Museum_of_Athens_on_14_April_2018_(cropped).jpg

What Happened to the Statue of Zeus?

Once majestically towering over the picturesque Greek Peloponnese Peninsula, the Temple of Zeus served as a sacred space for worship. Athletes from all over would gather every four years on this hallowed ground, paying homage to the gods, making offerings to Zeus, and pledging their commitment to fair play before engaging in the competitions. The temple played a significant role in honoring Zeus and facilitating the grand athletic festivities that captivated participants and spectators.

According to Roman historian Suetonius, Roman Emperor Caligula, who reigned from 37 to 41 CE, wanted the Statue of Zeus to be relocated to Rome since the statue was so grand. However, he also wanted to take off Zeus's head and replace it with his own. This story might not be real, but this next part is pure fiction. When Caligula died in 41, the statue apparently knew, as it burst into laughter, causing the scaffolding to crumble.

Although Caligula did not bring about the statue's end, it did meet a gruesome fate. Like the Temple of Artemis, Christianity played a large role in the temple's and statue's demise. In 393 CE, Emperor Theodosius I issued a decree banning the Olympic Games. There is archaeological evidence that the games continued, although they were not as grand as they once were. That changed under Theodosius II, who was even more ruthless in rooting out paganism. He ordered the destruction of the Temple of Zeus in Olympia in 426 CE.

It takes a lot to ruin a grand temple, though, and it is likely pieces of it still stood after the dust had fallen and the flames had subsided. Whatever was left would have been affected by the earthquakes that shook the land in 522 and 551 CE. After a bad flood, the area was abandoned, with silt and other organic materials burying the temple. The Temple of Zeus wouldn't be remembered by history until 1766 when Richard Chandler, an English historian, identified it. Excavations of the site would take place around sixty years later.

The statue would not have been as hard to tear apart as the temple itself. But it is hard to know for sure what exactly happened to it. In 391, Emperor Theodosius I banned pagan worship and closed the temples. People might have taken advantage of that order to tear the statue apart, with pieces of it being melted down to sell. It might have been torn apart and carted off to somewhere else where it was put back together.

Historians once believed it was taken to Constantinople, where it was later destroyed in a fire in 475.

If it wasn't removed prior to the temple's destruction in 425, the statue would have been destroyed then. And if that was the case, it likely was destroyed by people who fervently believed in Christianity or the emperor, or it burned in the fire.

The Temple of Zeus at Olympia, once a shining symbol of religious devotion and a venue for grand athletic celebrations, now exists merely as ruins. Nevertheless, the memory of this extraordinary temple and the captivating Statue of Zeus it sheltered continues to ensnare the imagination and inspire artists today.

An illustration of the Statue of Zeus.
https://commons.wikimedia.org/wiki/File:Le_Jupiter_Olympien_ou_l%27art_de_la_sculpture_antique.jpg

Summary of Events

- 776 BCE: First athletic games take place at Olympia to honor Zeus.

- c. 456 BCE: The Temple of Zeus at Olympia is constructed.

- 435 BCE - The Statue of Zeus is created by Phidias. This masterpiece is recognized as one of the Seven Wonders of the Ancient World.

- 225 BCE: Philo of Byzantium documents the Seven Wonders of the Ancient World, which included the Statue of Zeus at Olympia.

- 395 CE: The statue of Zeus at Olympia is supposedly relocated to Constantinople.

- 426 CE: Emperor Theodosius II orders the destruction of the Temple of Zeus at Olympia.

- 475 CE: The Statue of Zeus is destroyed in a fire in Constantinople.[4]

---

[4] It must be noted that there is no firm proof of what happened to the Statue of Zeus. This is just one of the theories.

Chapter 5 – The Mausoleum of Halicarnassus

The Mausoleum of Halicarnassus, also referred to as the Tomb of Mausolus, was a shrine dedicated to Mausolus and his wife and sister, Artemisia II of Caria (present-day Turkey). This relationship was out of place, as there is no mention of Carian rulers practicing incest. Some scholars believe the marriage was symbolic, especially since the two never had children. Mausolus and Artemisia II served as governors (satraps) in the Persian Empire.

Who Was Mausolus?

Mausolus was a Persian satrap in the region of Caria, situated in the southwestern part of Anatolia. His rule lasted from either 377 or 376 to his demise in 353 BCE. He was born in Caria and fostered an ambitious vision of elevating his domain to the status of an expansionist power, prompting him to relocate his capital from Mylasa to the coastal city of Halicarnassus.

Intriguingly, Mausolus played a pivotal role in the momentous revolt staged by the Anatolian satraps against the formidable Persian king Artaxerxes II. Yet, demonstrating an astute sense of timing, Mausolus wisely withdrew from the conflict before succumbing to defeat. This maneuver allowed him to preserve his autonomy as a ruler and further solidify his influence over the territories under his sway.

Notably, Mausolus incorporated fragments of Lycia and several Ionian Greek cities into his expanding domain. In an act of strategic alliance, he provided support to the islands of Rhodes, Cos, and Chios in their struggle against mighty Athens, culminating in their resounding victory. Consequently, Rhodes and Cos fell under Mausolus's sphere of influence, further augmenting his political power.

Halicarnassus blossomed into a thriving capital city under Mausolus's guidance. Driven by a vision of impregnable security, he undertook extensive fortification projects, constructing formidable defensive walls, watchtowers, and three distinct walled citadels. These architectural endeavors served as a testament to his sagacity and tangible manifestations of his unwavering commitment to safeguarding his realm.

Mausolus's reign bore witness to a unique dynamic, as he shared the reins of power with his sister and wife, Artemisia II. This arrangement was unconventional, to say the least. There is no mention of incest being popular in Caria, and it seems unlikely the two ever consummated their marriage. Artemisia also held some power, even though she herself was not referred to as a satrap. Together, the couple steered Caria and its neighboring territories through twenty-four eventful years.

In regard to the subject of this section, Mausolus initiated the construction of an awe-inspiring sepulcher that would subsequently be known as the Mausoleum of Halicarnassus, a marvel listed among the Seven Wonders of the Ancient World. Upon his demise, Artemisia assumed the mantle of overseeing the completion of this grand tomb, which featured larger-than-life depictions of the Carian king and queen. This architectural project was a collaborative effort conceived by Greek architects named Pythius and Satyrus (also spelled as Satyros) and embellished by the masterful hands of esteemed Greek sculptors like Scopas, Bryaxis, Leochares, and Timotheus.

Mausolus left an enduring legacy that extended far and wide. He is known for being a tyrannical ruler by the Greeks he ruled, but his territorial expansions brought Caria unprecedented growth, while his unwavering support for commerce and fortification engendered prosperity and security. His steadfast promotion of Greek culture and literature fostered an atmosphere of intellectualism within his domain.

The term "mausoleum" became an enduring testament to Mausolus, with the term being used to refer to any imposing burial structure. Although the physical remnants of the mausoleum now lie in ruins, the profound impact of his reign on Caria and the splendor of his architectural masterpiece continue to mesmerize historians and visitors alike.

Who Was Artemisia II?

Artemisia II acted as a ruler, patron, and scholar. She was born circa 395 BCE as the eldest daughter of Hecatomnus, the first of his line as a Carian satrap. Her other siblings included Mausolus, Ada, Idrieus, and Pixodarus. Ada and Idrieus would also marry each other, likely to solidify Idrieus as the next satrap of Caria, similar to Artemisia II and Mausolus.

Artemisia played a pivotal role in consolidating her family's claim to a relatively autonomous Caria while honoring the overarching authority of the Persian Empire. Collaborating with her husband Mausolus, she masterfully thwarted Athenian imperial aspirations embodied in the Second Delian Confederacy, safeguarding Caria's cherished autonomy.

Tragedy struck Artemisia's life with the demise of her husband and brother in 353 BCE, compelling her to devote the remainder of her existence to immortalizing his memory. It is likely that Mausolus had already planned a grand tomb to be built, but Artemisia was the one who saw it come to life. She oversaw the construction of Mausolus's mausoleum, an opulent burial complex that would grace the city of Halicarnassus (modern-day Bodrum, Turkey). This architectural marvel, revered for its grandeur and splendor, ascended to the prestigious ranks of the Seven Wonders of the Ancient World, magnetizing travelers with its allure.

The profound grief that enveloped Artemisia's heart following her husband's passing permeated her every breath until her own demise in 351 BCE. It is even said that she drank her brother's ashes because she was so distraught. She hired poets to praise his name, and she ensured the mausoleum would be finished to honor Mausolus's greatness.

Her reign as Caria's sole ruler endured a mere two years, culminating in her brother Idrieus and sister Ada jointly ascending to the throne. The mantle of power was then passed on to their younger brother, Pixodarus, in 340 BCE.

Beyond Artemisia's political triumphs, she also explored the realms of botany and medicine. She engaged in research and garnered some acclaim. In fact, a drug used to help treat malaria, Artemisinin, was named after the plant Artemisia annua, which was named after Artemisia II.

Artemisia II is remembered as a devoted spouse, influential ruler, and revered patroness of the arts who bequeathed an enduring legacy through the magnificent Mausoleum of Halicarnassus. Her indomitable spirit and unwavering dedication continue to resonate with people today, making the study of the Mausoleum of Halicarnassus all the more interesting.

An Architectural Marvel: The Mausoleum of Halicarnassus

The construction of the mausoleum, situated in Halicarnassus (present-day Bodrum, Turkey), took place between 353 and 350 BCE. This impressive structure, reaching an estimated height of approximately 148 feet (45 meters), was the collaborative effort of two Greek architects, Satyrus and Pythius. Adding to its grandeur, five renowned Greek sculptors of the time, Bryaxis, Leochares, Scopas, Timotheus, and Pythius (who was also involved in crafting the chariot), contributed to the design of each of its four sides.

Halicarnassus was founded by the Dorians, with its origins dating back before 1100 BCE, although historians have not reached a consensus on the exact founding date. By the time Mausolus assumed power, the region had undergone significant changes. It was no longer a Dorian colony but had become part of the vast Persian Empire. Despite this, Mausolus, who inherited the position of satrap of Caria from his father in 377 or 376 BCE, embraced Greek customs and governance. He transformed Halicarnassus into the new capital and worked diligently to showcase Greek architecture. Mausolus constructed streets and buildings for the local population and fortified the port with impressive structures. These efforts brought about substantial improvements to the city, including the creation of ports, a palace, and numerous temples, which stimulated trade in the eastern Mediterranean and bolstered the city's economy. Halicarnassus is also famous for being the birthplace of the renowned historian Herodotus, who was born in the 5th century BCE.

While Mausolus undoubtedly revitalized the city and expanded his influence, he was not universally regarded in a favorable light. Some individuals branded him a tyrant or despot due to his authoritarian rule. In 353 BCE, Mausolus passed away, leaving Artemisia II devastated. To honor her late husband, Artemisia decided to move ahead with his plans to erect an extraordinary tomb. Despite facing a rebellion from the Greek island of Rhodes following Mausolus's death, Artemisia managed to secure the necessary funds and dispatched five exceptional sculptors to oversee the construction of the tomb. Regrettably, Artemisia died a mere two years later, shortly before the mausoleum was finished. Both of their remains were interred within the incomplete mausoleum. This hilltop structure, adorned with stone lions and soldiers, featured thirty-six columns.

Tragically, the mausoleum's fate took a turn when a series of earthquakes struck between the 12th and 15th centuries CE, reducing it to ruins. The remnants of this once-majestic monument were later repurposed in the construction of other buildings, including the castle built by the Knights of Saint John, also known as the Knights Hospitaller. Nevertheless, fragments of statues and slabs from the mausoleum have found a new home in the British Museum in London, England.

Even today, grieving families continue to erect mausoleums as eternal resting places for their departed loved ones. Perhaps the most renowned mausoleum worldwide, and incidentally one of the Seven Wonders of the New World, is the Taj Mahal.

A model of what the Mausoleum of Halicarnassus might have looked like.
Jona Lendering, CC0, via Wikimedia Commons;
https://commons.wikimedia.org/wiki/File:Mausoleum_at_Halicarnassus_at_the_Bodrum_Museu m_of_Underwater_Archaeology.jpg

So, What Did the Mausoleum Look Like?

The Mausoleum of Halicarnassus was an imposing edifice built to serve as the final resting place for Mausolus and Artemisia. It radiated an air of exceptional grandeur and lavishness. Its dimensions, though not precisely known, can be deduced from historical accounts and archaeological discoveries that attest to its colossal and opulent character.

Perched on a stone platform nestled within a courtyard, the mausoleum was adorned with an array of sculptures, including statues depicting gods, goddesses, and lions. The central tomb, shaped like a truncated pyramid, ascended in the form of a nearly square cube, measuring approximately 126 feet by 106 feet (38.4 meters by 32.5 meters). Adorning the base of the structure was an intricate bas-relief frieze, displaying intricate artistry.

Enclosed within a protective barrier, the mausoleum featured an east-facing chamber, serving both as a functional vestibule and a symbolic threshold between the realm of the living and the domain of the departed. This demarcation of the temporal and spiritual realms through dedicated spaces was a customary practice in antiquity and carried deep cultural significance.

Thirty-six columns provided support to the mausoleum's roof, with ten columns adorning each side and one gracing each corner. These columns matched the height of the roof, which took the form of a pyramid, complete with twenty-four steps. At the pinnacle of the mausoleum, an illustrious quadriga statue commanded attention. A quadriga is a portrayal of four horses pulling a chariot; in this case, the quadriga was possibly transporting Mausolus and Artemisia to the heavens.

Though the exact measurements remain shrouded in uncertainty, historians frequently reference the figures provided by Pliny the Elder, who cited a total perimeter of 411 feet (125 meters). Gaius Julius Hyginus alluded to the mausoleum's resplendent stone embellishments and approximate dimensions as being 80 feet (24 meters) in height and 1,340 feet (410 meters) in circumference.

The interior of the mausoleum housed an expansive collection of sculptures, boasting over four hundred free-standing statues painstakingly crafted by master artists. The walls were adorned with a plethora of reliefs and friezes, displaying diverse aspects of Mausolus's life and the pivotal events of his time. Bearing the influences of Greek culture, these friezes also depicted epic battles between the Greeks and the Amazons, as well as the clashes between the Greeks and the Centaurs.

These extravagant embellishments, epitomized by the larger-than-life statues, would have made the Mausoleum of Halicarnassus truly awe-inspiring, creating an atmosphere of profound reverence and admiration. While its precise measurements may elude us, there is no doubt that this structure stood as a monumental testament to the elevated status and immense power wielded by Mausolus and Artemisia.

An example of one of the friezes that could be found in the mausoleum. This is the Amazonomachy Relief and shows two Amazons, three Greeks, and a horse duking it out.
Carole Raddato; Attribution-ShareAlike 2.0 Generic (CC BY-SA 2.0);
https://creativecommons.org/licenses/by-sa/2.0/; https://www.flickr.com/photos/carolemage/16897971954/

The Quadriga

As mentioned, the Mausoleum of Halicarnassus was adorned with a massive statue referred to as the quadriga, which sat atop the structure. A quadriga was a type of two-wheeled chariot pulled by four horses. The statue was approximately 21 feet (6.5 meters) in length and stood at a height of around 16.5 feet (5 meters). The quadriga did not remain intact, but fragments of it can still be seen today at the British Museum. One of the fragmented horses has its head lifted high and turned to the left, which imparts a sense of energy and vitality.

One of the horses of the Quadriga of the Mausoleum of Halicarnassus. It became fragmented over the centuries.

https://commons.wikimedia.org/wiki/File:Horse_Halicarnassus_BM_1002.jpg

The horse was intricately carved, as you can see its muscles and veins. Its teeth and tongue were also skillfully carved. The mane covers both sides of the horse's neck, and there is a lock of hair around its right eye. Two strips of a harness wrap around the torso, connecting the collar to the crest of the headgear. Remnants of paint are still visible, and the statue in its modern form was reconstructed using various parts.

It is not known for sure what the quadriga was meant to represent. Some scholars believe that it was inspired by a religious funeral rite. It is believed Mausolus and Artemisia were in the chariot, but it is not known for sure. If the chariot was empty, it is possible it was meant as an offering to Mausolus. This was a rare custom in ancient Greece, but it did occur on occasion.

Since it is more likely that the chariot was occupied, other theories have emerged. It makes sense that the chariot would have been occupied by Mausolus and Artemisia, with the quadriga being made in honor of them. However, it is also possible that the chariot was used by Mausolus and his driver. The Greek goddess of triumph, Nike, was often depicted accompanying a monarch on his way to the afterlife. Some scholars also believe that either the deity Helios or Apollo controlled the chariot.

What Happened to the Mausoleum of Halicarnassus?

Halicarnassus, with the mausoleum nestled within its embrace, bore witness to the relentless dance of earthquakes spanning centuries. The rhythmic undulations of these seismic disturbances inflicted wounds upon the mausoleum, gradually eroding its splendor and leaving behind ruins. The tremors bear the responsibility for the decay and ultimate collapse of the mausoleum. It is unknown if just one massive earthquake damaged the building or if successive earthquakes brought the building down.

In the annals of the 15ᵗʰ century CE, a chapter unfolds where the Knights of Saint John of Rhodes, better known as the Knights Hospitaller (their full name is the Order of Knights of the Hospital of Saint John of Jerusalem), embarked upon the construction of a fortress in Bodrum, melding the remnants of the Mausoleum of Halicarnassus into its fortifications. These gallant knights sought to erect an impregnable bastion, shielding the region from incursions and warding off any aggression.

It is important to note that by the time the Knights Hospitaller repurposed the mausoleum, it had already succumbed to ruin. The ceaseless quakes and the relentless march of time had exacted their toll upon the edifice, rendering it a dilapidated shell. The knights, resourceful as they were, employed the remnants of the once-majestic structure as a veritable quarry, gathering stones and materials to serve their own construction endeavors.

Next, we find ourselves transported to the 1850s CE amidst the excavations conducted under the stewardship of Charles Thomas Newton. Within the bowels of the earth, an opulent trove lay in wait, as countless artifacts and sculptures revealed themselves. Amongst the unveiled treasures were statues of ethereal beauty, frieze slabs that whispered tales of forgotten epochs, and sculpted figures immortalizing the regal splendor of lions and horses. These relics were carefully documented and transported, their journey leading many to find a new home within the halls of the British Museum in London, where they presently reside. These sculptures and other artifacts offer a tantalizing glimpse into the artistry and architectural opulence that once enrobed the mausoleum.

It is worth noting that Charles Thomas Newton narrated a thrilling moment of discovering pieces of a horse statue. This remarkable find sparked an astonishing collaboration between eighty individuals hailing from the region, who valiantly united to transport the piece atop a sturdy sled. The walls encircling the area where this magnificent equine treasure was unearthed bear exquisite paintings.

However, the archaeologists did not find an accompanying chariot. Historical records concerning the discovery in Bodrum do not explicitly mention the unearthing of a chariot alongside the majestic horse's remains.

Yet, the fates of Mausolus and Artemisia, who were enshrined within the mausoleum, remain an elusive riddle. Though it is widely believed that their remains were interred within the sanctum, the precise coordinates of their tombs elude scholars. The earthquakes and the ensuing modifications to the structure have helped to shroud their final resting place. Perhaps their remains were destroyed, or perhaps we will one day discover them.

The castle that arose from the visionary ambitions of the Knights Hospitaller still adorns the landscape to this very day. Today, it is known as Bodrum Castle or the Castle of Saint Peter. Over the course of its existence, this fortress has witnessed numerous changes. Today, the Museum of Underwater Archaeology stands as a testament to the castle's enduring legacy. And there, within the sheltered confines of the castle's bastions, are the remnants of the Mausoleum of Halicarnassus, bridging the chasm between the past and the present and offering a tantalizing glimpse into the resplendence that once graced the city of Halicarnassus.

While the Mausoleum of Halicarnassus now lies as a modest mound of earth adorned with scattered stones and columns, its past grandeur never fails to captivate our collective imagination. This extraordinary architectural marvel rivaled even the famed pyramids of Giza. Its weathered remains stand as a testament to the ingenuity and artistic prowess of ancient civilizations, beckoning us to ponder the mysteries of the past and immerse ourselves in the rich tapestry of Bodrum's storied heritage.

Summary of Events

- 377/376 BCE–353 BCE: Mausolus rules over the kingdom of Caria.
- 353 BCE–350 BCE: Construction commences on the Mausoleum of Halicarnassus, which is intended to be the final resting place for Mausolus and his sister-wife, Artemisia II.[5]
- 225 BCE: Philo of Byzantium becomes the first known historian to mention the Seven Wonders of the Ancient World.
- Between the 12th century and the late 14th century CE: A devastating earthquake strikes, resulting in the tragic destruction of the Mausoleum of Halicarnassus, leaving behind mere remnants of its once-majestic splendor. It is possible that several earthquakes hit the region during this time.
- c. 1494 CE: The Knights of Saint John of Rhodes repurpose sections of the Mausoleum of Halicarnassus in the construction of the walls of Saint Peter's Castle in Bodrum.

---

[5] Many historians think a mausoleum of this size and detail would have taken longer to build. It is possible that its construction began earlier during Mausolus's rule or that later rulers helped finish it.

Chapter 6 – The Colossus of Rhodes

The Colossus of Rhodes embodied the grandeur of Greek mythology and the triumph of the human spirit. This monumental statue, which stood tall as a tribute to the radiant Greek sun god Helios, held a deeper significance rooted in history. Its creation is attributed to the brilliant mind of Chares of Lindos, and it was constructed between 292 and 280 BCE against the backdrop of Rhodes's glorious victory over Demetrius I Poliorcetes. The besieged city emerged victorious in 305 BCE, marking a turning point in its narrative.

Crafted with meticulous artistry, the Colossus of Rhodes left onlookers in awe. As legends tell, this colossal figure reached an astonishing height of approximately 110 feet (33.5 meters). Its core structure, concealed within a blend of bronze and iron, provided the necessary support to bear the weight of the sculpted stone exterior. These details are sadly all that is left of this ancient wonder.

Contemplating the exact whereabouts of the Colossus has also been a matter of intrigue and speculation. While historical records are scarce, the prevailing belief suggests that the statue graced the harbor, commanding the attention of all who approached. This location, a gateway to the thriving city of Rhodes, would have allowed visitors to bask in the awe-inspiring presence of the statue and possibly even sail between its legs as they entered the port city.

However, it is important to note that the accounts we have inherited from the Middle Ages very well might be inaccurate. Myths and legends were intertwined with history, blurring the lines between fact and fiction. So, while the portrayal of the Colossus as a towering sentinel overlooking the harbor evokes some vivid imagery, it is not known for sure if it stood there.

Nonetheless, one cannot dismiss the inherent allure of the Colossus of Rhodes. Even in the absence of precise details, the idea of a colossal monument dedicated to a revered deity speaks to the aspirations and achievements of humanity. Its inclusion among the Seven Wonders of the Ancient World exemplifies the magnitude of its impact and the enduring fascination it evokes.

Where Is Rhodes?

Rhodes, an island nestled in the Aegean Sea, holds a historical gem known as the port of Rhodes. Positioned at the northern tip of this landmass, the port played a pivotal role as a destination along various trade routes. These routes intertwined Greek cities in Asia Minor, such as Miletus, with the resplendent treasures of Egypt. The island of Rhodes itself is a fascinating place, steeped in history and rich in cultural heritage.

The ties between Rhodes and the illustrious city of Alexandria were as strong as the sturdy columns that adorned the magnificent temples of old. The year 331 BCE was a momentous year in history, for that was the year the mighty Alexander the Great established the city of Alexandria. This vibrant metropolis became a beacon of culture and knowledge, captivating the hearts and minds of those who ventured there.

Even in more recent times, Rhodes has continued to captivate visitors with its picturesque landscapes and idyllic beaches. The Old Town, a UNESCO World Heritage Site, stands as a testament to the island's medieval past, with its imposing fortifications, narrow cobbled streets, and charming blend of Byzantine, Ottoman, and Italian influences.

The Rhodian Conflict

The ancient city of Rhodes held a significant position in the realm of commerce, owing to its strategic location along major trade routes. During the reign of Alexander the Great's successors, the Mediterranean region flourished, attracting the attention of influential figures like Demetrius I of Macedon, who was entrusted by his father, Antigonus I, a former comrade of Alexander, to conquer vast territories. When Alexander died, his vast empire fragmented, with his generals fighting for control over it. Antigonus ultimately ruled over Macedonia and its neighboring domains.

In 306 BCE, before assuming kingship, Antigonus dispatched his son, Demetrius, to launch an assault on Ptolemy, another of Alexander's generals who later established his dominion over Egypt. Realizing the need for assistance, Demetrius sought the aid of the Rhodians, but they declined to lend their support. Demetrius still managed to emerge victorious, decimating Ptolemy's forces in the Battle of Salamis and subsequently annexing Cyprus.

This triumph was followed by a succession of coronations. Antigonus and his son declared themselves kings, and they were joined by Ptolemy, Cassander, Lysimachus, and Seleucus I Nicator, all of whom had served under Alexander. With newfound autonomy, Demetrius resolved to punish Rhodes by laying siege to its namesake capital.

Rhodes, the administrative center of the island, found itself encircled by Demetrius, who amassed a force of around forty thousand soldiers and pirates. This number significantly surpassed the city's population, though it should be noted that ancient historians, while our main sources, occasionally embellished facts for dramatic effect or propagandistic motives. Nonetheless, it remains plausible that Demetrius commanded a formidable assembly.

Engineers from far and wide were recruited to conceive and construct a remarkable siege weapon, a towering 125-foot (38-meter) structure equipped with wheels and housing a catapult. To safeguard the catapult operators, leather shutters were installed, and each level of the tower featured its own water tank in anticipation of the city's fiery counterattacks. Pushing this behemoth required over three thousand soldiers, but despite its awe-inspiring design and technological advancements, its effectiveness was nullified by the muddy surroundings caused by residential flooding in Rhodes. Demetrius also possessed an immense 180-foot (55-meter) battering ram, which required the efforts of approximately one thousand men to wield it effectively.

The conflict between Demetrius and the resolute people of Rhodes endured for an entire year until a ceasefire was negotiated. The citizens of Rhodes withstood the siege with unwavering determination, and when reinforcements from Egypt under Ptolemy's command arrived,

Demetrius had no alternative but to retreat from the island. Although he considered the siege a triumph due to Rhodes agreeing not to support Egypt in his war against Ptolemy, the tenacity of the Rhodians ultimately prevailed.

In the aftermath, the people of Rhodes found themselves in possession of Demetrius's colossal siege tower and other equipment, which they sold for a hefty profit. They decided to use the funds for the construction of a monumental statue in honor of their patron deity, Helios. And the rest, as they say, is history.

The Colossus of Rhodes

According to Greek mythology, Helios was the son of the Titans Hyperion and Theia and was venerated as the sun god by the Greeks. The Halieia festival, which honored Helios, was one of the most important religious celebrations on the island of Rhodes. The mythology of Rhodes is also tied to Helios through the nymph Rhodos, who was said to have been the mother of his sons.

The Colossus of Rhodes, a 110-foot statue of the Greek god Helios, was built between 292 and 280 BCE. According to Roman historian Pliny the Elder, it took three hundred talents (an estimated five million dollars today) and twelve years to complete the project. It is unknown how many men worked on it, but the number was likely high. The statue had a bronze exterior and an iron framework. It was supported by two or three stone columns inside. The iron framework and stone columns were connected using iron rods.

Helios is typically depicted wearing a crown of sunbeams on silver coins during the Hellenistic period, so it is assumed that the statue bore the same appearance. Although the exact appearance and location of the statue are unknown, it is widely believed to have been located near the harbor. There are detractors to this theory, though. The statue is traditionally believed to have straddled the harbor, with the waterway passing under its legs. There are several remnants around the harbor that could have been the statue (none of which straddle the harbor). Although the idea of the Colossus of Rhodes straddling the harbor evokes a powerful image, it is incredibly unlikely that it did since it doesn't make sense from an engineering standpoint. Additionally, some scholars believe the Colossus of Rhodes was part of the Acropolis of Rhodes, which sat on a hill near the port. However, nothing has been confirmed so far, as there are no firm details of the statue's appearance or location.

Attempts have been made to rebuild the Colossus of Rhodes, with the first proposal presented in the 1970s. However, the rebuilding has been controversial. Some argue that it would boost the tourism industry, while others claim that it would cost hundreds of millions to recreate. In November 2008, it was announced that the statue would be reconstructed, but the exact height of the sculpture has not been determined. So far, the statue has not been built. One of the most recent proposals was in 2015, but plans have not moved forward.

How Was the Statue Constructed?

Modern architects and scholars widely acknowledge the existence of the Colossus of Rhodes, yet there persists an ongoing debate regarding how it was constructed. Chares of Lindos, a pupil of the renowned sculptor Lysippus, who held the esteemed position as Alexander the Great's personal sculptor, was assigned to the task. Tragically, Chares of Lindos met an untimely demise before completing the project. It is not known for certain how he died, which paved the way for myths and tales to come up with solutions. Some stories suggest that suicide was the cause. According to one account, a Rhodian inspected Chares's work and discovered a flaw that so overwhelmed the sculptor with shame that he resorted to taking his own life. Another story attributes Chares's suicide to his underestimation of the exorbitant cost involved in constructing such a colossal statue, leading him into bankruptcy and despair. However, historical records fail to definitively confirm the exact cause of his demise or whether he passed away prior to the statue's completion, although it is widely believed he died before it was finished.

Speculation also abounds when it comes to the construction method employed for the Colossus of Rhodes. One theory put forth by some scholars posits that Chares of Lindos used a large earthen ramp that expanded in size as the statue grew taller. This ramp would have allowed the workers access to the statue throughout the construction process. However, this idea finds little favor among modern architects, who consider it impractical and unrealistic, given the immense size and weight of the statue.

Constructing the Colossus of Rhodes undoubtedly presented formidable challenges due to its sheer scale and complexity. Unfortunately, no comprehensive records or architectural plans have survived to provide definitive insights into the specific techniques employed. As a result, architects and historians have to rely on ancient accounts and limited archaeological evidence to come up with their own conjectures regarding the construction process.

While contemporary architects continue to put forth theories and ideas, a widely accepted consensus on the construction of the Colossus of Rhodes remains elusive. The lack of conclusive evidence, coupled with the passage of time, contributes to the enduring mystery surrounding the methods employed in creating this monumental ancient masterpiece.

What Did the Statue Look Like?

The Colossus of Rhodes is indeed a fascinating subject, and while there is no extant description of the statue, there have been various theories proposed regarding its appearance. Based on the available information, it is believed that the Colossus stood approximately 110 feet tall, a number that includes its 50-foot stone pedestal.

The most widely accepted theory suggests that the statue depicted the Greek sun god Helios. It is thought that the statue portrayed a male figure with his arms raised in the air. Similar to the Statue of Liberty, which was erected centuries later, the Colossus of Rhodes is believed to have worn a crown of rays and potentially held a cloth or torch.

As we also mentioned, the location of where the Colossus stood is still a matter of debate. While it is commonly assumed that it was located near the harbor, the exact spot is not well documented. The idea that the statue straddled the harbor, as depicted in Martin van Heemskerck's 16th-century engraving, is now considered a misconception. Such a pose would have been deemed undignified for a god, and the construction required for such a stance would have likely necessitated the closure of the port for an extended period. It is now believed that the Colossus of Rhodes stood with its legs together.

We bring that point up again to highlight the similarities between the Colossus of Rhodes and the Statue of Liberty. Both statues were located near a harbor and depicted figures with raised arms, wearing a crown of rays and holding a torch. However, it is important to note that the Statue of Liberty was not directly inspired by the Colossus of Rhodes. Instead, it was a gift from France to the United States and was designed to symbolize freedom and democracy.

A 16th-century engraving of the Colossus of Rhodes by Martin van Heemskerck, who illustrated all of the Seven Wonders of the Ancient World.
https://en.wikipedia.org/wiki/File:Colossus_of_Rhodes.jpg

While the Colossus of Rhodes no longer exists, it continues to captivate our imagination, and the details of its appearance remain a subject of speculation and scholarly debate.

This engraving was created around 1875 by Sidney Barclay. It gives you another idea of what the statue might have looked like.
https://commons.wikimedia.org/wiki/File:Colosse_de_Rhodes_(Barclay).jpg

The Collapse of the Colossus of Rhodes

The Colossus of Rhodes stood for an impressive span of approximately fifty-six years until a mighty earthquake struck the region in 226 BCE (some sources also suggest it might have fallen during an earthquake in 228 BCE). Legend tells a tale of the Egyptian monarch Ptolemy III extending a generous offer to finance the reconstruction of the colossal sculpture. However, the inhabitants of Rhodes, guided by an oracle's enigmatic counsel, opted to forgo this opportunity.

Their unwavering conviction stemmed from a belief that the imposing statue had, in some way, incurred the wrath of the sun god Helios. In an extraordinary display of reverence, the Rhodians resolved to preserve the shattered remnants of the monument, allowing them to bear witness to the indomitable might of their celestial deity. As a testament to his immense power, the broken fragments of the Colossus lay scattered along the sun-kissed beaches of Rhodes, serving as a poignant reminder of its former magnificence.

The sands of time continued their ceaseless dance, and Rhodes experienced yet another chapter of transformation. In the year 654 CE, the island succumbed to the conquest of the Arab forces, which were led by the future founder of the Umayyad Caliphate, Mu'awiyah I. The chronicles of Theophanes the Confessor, a Byzantine historian of notable repute, narrate a captivating account of a Jewish merchant hailing from Edessa, an ancient city nestled in upper Mesopotamia. According to Theophanes, this astute trader purchased the fractured remains of the Colossus of Rhodes and undertook an arduous journey to transport his valuable acquisition.

Theophanes, ever the weaver of tales, asserts that an astonishing caravan of nine hundred camels bore the weight of this remarkable bounty. Alas, in the realm of historical inquiry, the veil of ambiguity shrouds this story, leaving us with little concrete evidence to substantiate its veracity. One might ponder why the Arab conquerors, who would have been eager to capitalize on selling the coveted metal, would willingly part with such a treasure rather than employ it for their own ambitious purposes.

Even if destiny had granted the Colossus of Rhodes an opportunity to rise anew, its triumph would have likely remained short-lived. Rhodes endured the wrath of numerous seismic upheavals after the cataclysmic tremor of 226 BCE. Moreover, with the advent of Christianity as the dominant force in the region, the inhabitants of Rhodes would have been disinclined to allocate their precious resources toward reconstructing a monument venerating a pagan deity.

Still, the Colossus of Rhodes, an emblem of the island's affluence and influence, became etched within the annals of history. The embellished accounts and descriptions of this architectural marvel rightfully propelled it to secure a coveted position among the illustrious Seven Wonders of the Ancient World.

Summary of Events

- 292–280 BCE: The Colossus of Rhodes, one of the Seven Wonders of the Ancient World, was constructed to represent the sun god Helios in the harbor of Rhodes.

- 228 or 226 BCE: The Colossus of Rhodes fell due to an earthquake.

- c. 225 BCE: Philo of Byzantium became the first recorded historian to mention the Seven Wonders of the Ancient World.

- c. 654 CE: According to Theophanes, a Jewish merchant transported the pieces of the destroyed Colossus of Rhodes to Edessa to be melted down.

Chapter 7 – The Lighthouse of Alexandria

The Lighthouse of Alexandria emerges from the annals of history with an air of majesty and intrigue. Revered as the Pharos of Alexandria, this architectural marvel is said to have graced the island of Pharos, casting its radiant light near the bustling harbor of Alexandria. Imposing in its grandeur, the lighthouse soared to awe-inspiring heights, surpassing over 350 feet (110 meters).

By delving deep into the chronicles of time, we find ourselves transported to the reigns of Ptolemy I and Ptolemy II, which was when this extraordinary beacon first illuminated the Egyptian sky. It was during this same century that the city of Alexandria was envisioned by the conqueror Alexander the Great in the year 331 BCE.

Nestled alongside the gentle flow of the majestic Nile, Alexandria flourished as a hub of trade and commerce. The city boasted not one but two natural harbors, luring merchants from distant lands to its shores. In 305 BCE, under the astute rule of Ptolemy I, Alexandria became the capital of the Ptolemaic dynasty, her influence stretching far and wide across the realm.

And Alexandria's allure extended beyond its economic prowess. A tapestry of cultures walked its vibrant streets, with wanderers and explorers being drawn to the city from every corner of Greece and beyond. In this captivating melting pot of diversity, knowledge, and wisdom, the people found fertile ground to advance the arts, education, and much else.

Alexandria minted its own currency, a testament to its independence and economic prowess. Coins bearing the city's mark served as symbols of trade, unity, and the march of progress. They bore witness to Alexandria's unique place in the tapestry of human civilization.

Today, Alexandria endures as a thriving metropolis, a testament to the resilience of human endeavors. Alexandria claims the honor of being Egypt's second-largest city, with the first being Cairo. The echoes of ancient wonders and the whispers of history permeate the air, inviting all who visit to be swept away by the indomitable allure of this timeless city.

Who Built the Lighthouse of Alexandria?

The construction of the Lighthouse of Alexandria was initiated by Ptolemy I, who reigned from 305 to 282 BCE. Ptolemy is notable for being one of Alexander the Great's generals and the founder of the Ptolemaic dynasty in Egypt. The exact timeline of its construction remains a topic of debate among historians, though. Some sources suggest that the initial construction of the lighthouse occurred around 300 BCE and that its completion took place possibly in 282 or 280 during the reign of Ptolemy II, who governed from 284 to 246 BCE.[6] Alternative theories propose that Ptolemy I commissioned the lighthouse but that the actual construction commenced in 284 and concluded in 246. The primary purpose of this monumental structure was twofold: to facilitate safe navigation for ships approaching the city and to proudly display Alexandria's opulence and grandeur to the world.

Overseeing the construction of the Lighthouse of Alexandria was Sostratus, an esteemed architect hailing from Cnidus, an ancient Greek city situated in Caria, which corresponds to modern-day Turkey. However, some sources say that Sostratus did not design the lighthouse but instead helped to finance the project. The lighthouse once perched atop the limestone islet on the island of Pharos, majestically surveying the bustling port city of Alexandria. This city boasted two distinct harbors, Eunostos and the Megas Limin, both of which benefited from the lighthouse's illuminating presence.

The Lighthouse of Alexandria was dedicated to Zeus, the king of the gods, and possibly the sea god Proteus. Proteus was known for ensuring

---

[6] You might notice that the regnal years of Ptolemy I and Ptolemy II don't match up. Ptolemy II was declared king by his father in 284 and served as his co-regent.

the safety of seafarers and was revered for his ability to guide ships through treacherous waters. Zeus was honored for his unwavering commitment to safeguarding sailors and providing them with direction during their perilous journeys. While it remains challenging to definitively establish whether lighthouses predate the Lighthouse of Alexandria, it still stands as the first recorded lighthouse in human history and the tallest one ever built.[7] After the Lighthouse of Alexandria was built, lighthouses proliferated throughout major Mediterranean cities, serving as beacons of hope for weary travelers and indispensable navigational aids. These towering structures played a pivotal role in identifying perilous reefs and hazardous rocks, offering protection to seafarers traversing the vast expanses of the sea.

A depiction of the Lighthouse of Alexandria (Pharos) by Philip Galle.
https://commons.wikimedia.org/wiki/File:Philip_Galle_-_Lighthouse_of_Alexandria_(Pharos_of_Alexandria)_-_1572.jpg

What Did the Lighthouse of Alexandria Look Like?

The Lighthouse of Alexandria, also known as the pharos, was an iconic structure located on the island of Pharos in Egypt. While the exact

---

[7] It must be noted that many lists don't count the Lighthouse of Alexandria on lists of the tallest lighthouses since it is possible the numbers were exaggerated.

details of its design are uncertain, historians believe that it consisted of three levels with distinct shapes. The first level was rectangular, the second level was octagonal, and the third level was spherical. These unique shapes were intended to set the lighthouse apart from other buildings in the area.

The island was connected to the mainland by a causeway called the Heptastadion, which spanned approximately 4,130 feet (1,260 meters). This causeway played a crucial role in providing access to the island and the lighthouse itself. Accounts by Arab writers suggest that the lighthouse had an interior stairway connecting each floor, as well as an external ramp.

Estimates of the lighthouse's height vary, with a range of 330 to 460 feet. However, the prevailing consensus among historians is that it stood around 350 feet tall, making it the tallest manmade structure of its time and the tallest lighthouse ever built. The lighthouse was constructed using light-colored stone, most likely white, to ensure its visibility as a navigational aid.

The exact lighting system of the lighthouse is a topic of debate. While some ancient sources do not mention the use of light, Pliny the Elder describes a flame in the lighthouse. It is believed that burning oil or papyrus was used to keep the upper part of the tower visible at night. There is uncertainty about whether this lighting system was present from the beginning, though. According to later Arab writers, a polished bronze mirror was used to reflect the flame and enhance its visibility at sea. The mirror could also be utilized to reflect sunlight during the day.

Limited information is available regarding statues or artwork associated with the lighthouse. Depictions on Roman imperial coinage show a tower with a colossal figure and two smaller figures of Triton blowing conch shells, but these depictions do not provide details about the lighthouse's interior or lighting system.

In recent times, underwater explorations have uncovered blocks from a submerged structure in Alexandria's harbor that potentially belong to the legendary lighthouse. However, scholars debate whether these blocks are from the lighthouse itself or from other structures that used repurposed materials.

Overall, while the Lighthouse of Alexandria's precise appearance and features remain elusive, it was an impressive architectural feat and an important symbol of ancient Alexandria.

The Lighthouse of Alexandria's Destruction

Throughout its tumultuous history, the Lighthouse of Alexandria bore the brunt of relentless earthquakes, their destructive force etching scars upon its towering form. The annals of time reveal fleeting glimpses into the specific ravages each earthquake wrought upon this magnificent structure, but comprehensive accounts remain scarce, shrouding the events in mystery. Undoubtedly, the passage of time has led to discrepancies in sources.

The earthquakes that reverberated through Alexandria in the years 796 CE, 951 CE, 956 CE, 1303 CE, and 1323 CE inflicted grave consequences upon the lighthouse. This majestic emblem of the city's opulence and maritime prowess suffered partial collapses and extensive damage.

Nevertheless, the lighthouse continued to shine, as time and time again, engineers and artisans sought to restore and possibly expand the building. They diligently toiled to resurrect the grandeur and functionality of this iconic structure, breathing life into it once more. Such meticulous repairs were undertaken to ensure that the beacon continued to guide and safeguard seafaring vessels navigating the treacherous waters of Alexandria's harbor.

In the annals of the Fatimid period, after the 956 earthquake destroyed part of the lighthouse, a transformative metamorphosis took hold of the structure. Atop its lofty edifice, an imposing dome materialized, an architectural testament to the adaptability and harmonious fusion of Islamic elements within the existing framework. This spiritual transformation endowed the lighthouse with renewed purpose, acting as a union of faith and functionality.

An intriguing linguistic connection unites the architectural design of the lighthouse with the minarets that punctuate the Arab landscape. In the Arabic language, the term for "lighthouse" is *manarah*. This alludes to the influence the lighthouse wielded over the development of minarets.

Yet, following the 14th century CE, the historical accounts abruptly cease talking about the lighthouse. It is widely believed that another cataclysmic earthquake, potentially unfurling its destructive forces in the 1330s CE, eventually sealed the lighthouse's fate. This seismic upheaval likely unleashed unparalleled devastation upon Alexandria.

The granite foundations of the lighthouse found a new purpose in the construction of the resplendent Qaitbay fortress during the 15ᵗʰ century CE. The fort incorporated the lighthouse's sturdy foundations, turning them into a new bastion of strength.

In the realm of maritime archaeology, explorers of bygone depths have unearthed a trove of fragmented stones and two monumental statues adorning the likeness of Ptolemy I and Queen Berenice, Ptolemy's wife. These precious relics, discovered in close proximity to the lighthouse's remnants, provide tangible evidence of the lighthouse's historical significance and offer a tantalizing glimpse into the past.

The exact number of ships saved by the lighthouse's beacon remains unknown, but it undoubtedly saved many. Alexandria's ancient harbor, a realm of treacherous currents and lurking perils, failed to offer sanctuary to seafarers, as evidenced by the discovery of over forty shipwrecks strewn amidst its depths. The lighthouse likely played a pivotal role in guiding vessels safely into the harbor's protective embrace, though the extent of its impact will never be known.

The Lighthouse of Alexandria bore witness to a tumultuous saga and was beset by unyielding earthquakes and the ravages of time. Yet, despite the scars etched upon its venerable façade, its enduring architectural and cultural legacy reverberates through history. Each restoration, each rebirth, and each lustrous chapter serves as a testament to the profound ingenuity that thrived within the hearts of the ancients, etching the name of the lighthouse in the annals of human achievement.

Summary of Events

- 300–246 BCE: The Lighthouse of Alexandria, one of the Seven Wonders of the Ancient World, is created.

- c. 225 BCE: Philo of Byzantium lists the Seven Wonders of the Ancient World.

- 956 CE: An earthquake caused the partial collapse of the Lighthouse of Alexandria. The top of the lighthouse was later replaced with an Islamic-style dome.

- c. 1330 CE: The Lighthouse of Alexandria finally collapses due to an earthquake.

Conclusion

The Seven Wonders of the Ancient World have captivated individuals for centuries, as they highlight the extraordinary complexity and sheer architectural brilliance that characterized human craftsmanship in antiquity. It is of the utmost importance to emphasize that these legendary lists, which encompass compilations by illustrious figures such as Herodotus, Callimachus of Cyrene, Antipater of Sidon, and Philo of Byzantium, stand as the conventional list that has been passed down through countless generations. Nevertheless, there are other remarkable structures that stand worthy of recognition alongside the wonders on the traditional list.

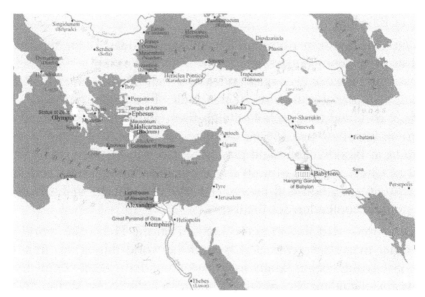

These are the sites of the Seven Wonders of the Ancient World. They were located in Greece, North Africa, and Asia Minor. Construction for these wonders lasted anywhere from 2550 BCE for the Great Pyramid of Giza to potentially 246 BCE for the Lighthouse of Alexandria. The dates for the construction of the wonders vary greatly. The Great Pyramid of Giza is the only ancient wonder on the traditional list that has survived to the present day. However, archaeological digs have uncovered many of the lost wonders of the ancient world, except for the Hanging Gardens of Babylon.

Several ancient lists include the walls of Babylon, an imposing structure that, according to the accounts of Herodotus, spanned a staggering fifty-six miles (ninety kilometers) in length, with select sections being eighty feet (twenty-four kilometers) thick. The wall was 320 feet (97 kilometers) tall! Modern historians think these estimates are exaggerations, but they do help to show how impressive the walls must have been. The walls of Babylon used to be on the traditional lists, but the Lighthouse of Alexandria took their place.

The influence of Christianity impacted later lists created by historians and scholars like Gregory of Tours. His list included sites like Noah's Ark (an ancient wonder on par with the Hanging Gardens of Babylon, for it is not known if it existed or where it was built), Solomon's Temple in Jerusalem, the Grave of the Persian King (it is not known what this refers to, although it is possible it refers to the Mausoleum of Halicarnassus), the Lighthouse of Alexandria, the Colossus of Rhodes, the theater of Heraclea (which was built into a rocky outcrop), and the walls of Babylon.

The Colosseum in Rome, which still stands today, often appears on the lists of ancient wonders, and it is easy to understand why. It was the largest amphitheater ever built and stands right in the center of Rome, making it impossible to miss. It was built of concrete, limestone, and volcanic rock and used to hold the gladiatorial games. It is believed that up to eighty thousand spectators once sat in the Colosseum's seats, watching as bloody battles and plays took place in the arena. The Great Wall of China, a series of walls that cover over thirteen thousand miles (over twenty-one thousand kilometers), and Stonehenge in England are also popular contenders for the list.

Some argue that the list is too focused on the Hellenistic world and that other marvels were created around the world during this time that were just as interesting. Many lists of wonders have been completed in the years, including the Seven Wonders of the New World (which actually includes the Colosseum and the Great Wall of China), the Seven Natural Wonders of the World, and the Seven Wonders of the Solar System, to name a few.

But let's turn back to the traditional list and take one last look at these marvels. The Great Pyramid of Giza still stands as a testament to the grandeur of ancient civilizations. It soared to unimaginable heights, its majestic form cloaked in the resplendent beauty of white limestone, rendering it a breathtaking sight under the sun. Around the pyramids lay the archaeological remnants of the Old Kingdom, unearthing compelling evidence of the rulers' military prowess and the kingdom's profound artistic achievements, further underscoring the legacy of this timeless wonder.

It is not known if the Hanging Gardens of Babylon existed, but its legacy endures all the same. It is exciting to think that the gardens might have once existed, and it is just as exciting diving into the theories about it. If it did exist, it was, no doubt, something truly marvelous to behold.

The resplendent Temple of Artemis in Ephesus claims its rightful place among the seven ancient wonders. Nestled near the tranquil embrace of the sea, this temple exuded an unparalleled allure. Pliny the Elder called it the most mesmerizing structure of the ancient Greek period. Pausanias, the esteemed Greek author of the 2nd century CE, further extolled its magnificence, asserting that it stood unrivaled as the pinnacle of human achievement, a marvel that left the world spellbound.

The inclusion of the Statue of Zeus speaks volumes about its enduring fame and universal recognition. Even before its formal acknowledgment on the list of seven ancient wonders, this grand statue had already etched its presence onto the artistic canvas of civilization, as it was immortalized in vase paintings, gemstones, and coins dating as far back as the 4th century BCE. Coins bearing the likeness of Alexander the Great and Roman Emperor Hadrian (r. 117-138 CE) bore witness to the widespread veneration of the Statue of Zeus, which was adorned with marble replicas of Niobe's offspring upon its regal throne.

The Mausoleum of Halicarnassus, with its colossal proportions and lavish embellishments, found its rightful place among the Seven Wonders of the Ancient World. The esteemed Greek historian Pausanias bestowed upon it the evocative name "Mausolea," an homage to its awe-inspiring size and the masterful sculptures that adorned its resplendent façade. Despite enduring several cataclysmic earthquakes, this imposing mausoleum reportedly remained steadfast until its fateful demise in the 13th century CE.

The Colossus of Rhodes, yet another marvel enshrined on the hallowed list, owed its inclusion to its breathtaking proportions. Originally, the ancient Greeks used the term "colossus" to designate statues of any size, but the construction of the Colossus of Rhodes transformed the word into a symbol of gargantuan magnitude. Sadly, the capricious hand of fate dealt a devastating blow to Rhodes in 228 or 226 BCE when a catastrophic earthquake laid waste to the city and its prized statue. Accounts by the venerable Greek geographer and author Strabo recount the solemn abandonment of the fallen statue, for the Oracle of Delphi foretold dire misfortune should it be reconstructed.

Lastly, the Lighthouse of Alexandria, resplendent in its uniqueness and towering stature, concludes the roster of the Seven Wonders of the Ancient World. Recognized for its distinctive design and soaring height, this remarkable edifice served as a beacon to guide mariners through treacherous waters. Its architectural blueprint, imbued with functional elegance, was emulated in other ancient civilizations, with lighthouses becoming a harbinger of safety and hope for seafarers navigating unfamiliar shores.

The allure of the Seven Wonders of the Ancient World has elicited many emotions and reactions throughout the years, stirring the hearts and minds of countless individuals. These resplendent marvels have served as a profound source of inspiration, compelling humanity to contemplate the magnificence and boundless potential of the human spirit when fueled by creativity, knowledge, and the unyielding determination to construct grand and remarkable structures. Undeniably, these seven wonders stand as a testament to the extraordinary feats of engineering and architectural design achieved by ancient civilizations. As the tides of time continue to shift and new frontiers of exploration unfold, we eagerly anticipate the revelations that await, unlocking the enigmatic wonders of the past with each passing discovery.

Here's another book by Captivating History that you might like

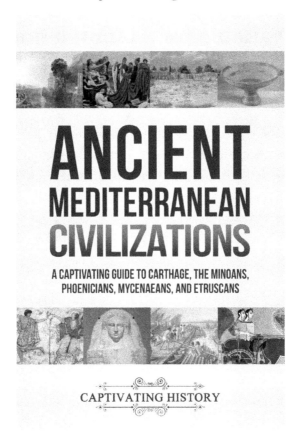

Free Bonus from Captivating History (Available for a Limited time)

Hi History Lovers!

Now you have a chance to join our exclusive history list so you can get your first history ebook for free as well as discounts and a potential to get more history books for free! Simply visit the link below to join.

Captivatinghistory.com/ebook

Also, make sure to follow us on Facebook, Twitter and Youtube by searching for Captivating History.

References

1. Ancient Greece. (n.d.). Zeus. Retrieved from https://ancient-greece.org/culture/mythology/zeus.html.

2. Art in Context. (n.d.). Statue of Zeus, Olympia. Retrieved from https://artincontext.org/zeus-statue-olympia/

3. Assmann, J. (2002). The Mind of Egypt: History and Meaning in the Time of the Pharaohs. New York: Metropolitan Books.

4. Barringer, J. (2007). What Happened to the Zeus of Olympia? The Annual of the British School at Athens, 102, 283-299. Retrieved from https://www.academia.edu/21863001/No_8_What_Happened_to_the_Zeus_of_Olympia_AHB_2007.

5. Best of Ephesus. (n.d.). Temple of Artemis. Retrieved from https://www.bestofephesus.com/temple-of-artemis.php

6. Britannica. (n.d.). Sennacherib. In Encyclopedia Britannica. Retrieved April 19, 2023, from https://www.britannica.com/biography/Sennacherib

7. Brown University. (n.d.). Greek Past: Zeus. Retrieved from https://www.brown.edu/Departments/Joukowsky_Institute/courses/greekpast/4868.html

8. Cartwright, M. (2018). "Colossus of Rhodes." Ancient History Encyclopedia. Retrieved from https://www.ancient.eu/Colossus_of_Rhodes/

9. Cartwright, M. (2018). "Hanging Gardens of Babylon." Ancient History Encyclopedia. Retrieved from https://www.ancient.eu/Hanging_Gardens_of_Babylon/

10. Cartwright, M. (2018). "Lighthouse of Alexandria." Ancient History Encyclopedia. Retrieved from https://www.ancient.eu/Lighthouse_of_Alexandria/

11. Cartwright, M. (2018). "Phidias." Ancient History Encyclopedia. https://www.ancient.eu/Phidias/

12. Cartwright, M. (2018). "Statue of Zeus at Olympia." Ancient History Encyclopedia. https://www.ancient.eu/Statue_of_Zeus_at_Olympia/

13. Cartwright, M., 2018. "Mausoleum at Halicarnassus." World History Encyclopedia. URL https://www.worldhistory.org/Mausoleum_at_Halicarnassus/ (accessed 11.1.22).

14. Cartwright, M., 2018. "Temple of Artemis at Ephesus." World History Encyclopedia. URL https://www.worldhistory.org/Temple_of_Artemis_at_Ephesus/ (accessed 11.1.22).

15. Dalley, S. (2013). The Mystery of the Hanging Garden of Babylon: An Elusive World Wonder Traced. Oxford University Press.

16. DK Find Out. (n.d.). Mausoleum of Halicarnassus. Retrieved from https://www.dkfindout.com/us/history/seven-wonders-world/mausoleum-halicarnassus/

17. Farrell, J. (n.d.). The Mother and Father of Greek Gods. University of Pennsylvania. Retrieved from http://ccat.sas.upenn.edu/~jfarrell/courses/myth/97/notes/mother_father.html

18. Faulkner, R. O. (1999). The Ancient Egyptian Pyramid Texts. Society of Biblical Literature.

19. Foster, J. (2005). Ancient Egypt: A Very Short Introduction. Oxford University Press.

20. Friedman, F. D. (2002). Egypt, Canaan, and Israel in Ancient Times. Princeton: Princeton University Press.

21. Greek Mythology. (n.d.). Artemis. Retrieved from https://www.greekmythology.com/Olympians/Artemis/artemis.html

22. Grout, J. (n.d.). Artemis. Retrieved from https://penelope.uchicago.edu/~grout/encyclopaedia_romana/greece/paganism/artemis.html.

23. Harris, Karen. (n.d.). Temple of Artemis: Destruction, Facts, Stories, Trivia. Retrieved from https://historydaily.org/temple-of-artemis-destruction-facts-stories-trivia

24. Hawass, Z. (2010). *Giza and the Pyramids: The Definitive History.* Cairo: Supreme Council of Antiquities Press.

25. Herodotus. (n.d.). The Histories. Retrieved from https://www.gutenberg.org/files/2707/2707-h/2707-h.htm

26. History.com, 2021. "Seven Wonders of the Ancient World." HISTORY. URL https://www.history.com/topics/ancient-history/seven-wonders-of-the-ancient-world (accessed 11.1.22).

27. Hornblower, S. (1982). *Mausolus.* Oxford, England: Oxford University Press.

28. Hyginus. (1938). *Fabulae.* Leipzig, Germany: Teubner.

29. Ikram, S. and Dodson, A. (eds.) (1998). *Beyond the Horizon: Studies in Egyptian Art, Archaeology, and History in Honour of Barry J. Kemp.* Cairo: American University in Cairo Press.

30. Jarus, Owen, 2022. "7 Wonders of the Ancient World". livescience.com. URL https://www.livescience.com/seven-wonders-of-the-ancient-world (accessed 11.1.22).

31. Jarus, Owen, 2022. "Pyramids of Giza & the Sphinx." livescience.com. URL https://www.livescience.com/22621-pyramids-giza-sphinx.html (accessed 11.1.22).

32. Josephus. *Against Apion*, Book 1, Chapter 20.

33. Lehner, M. (1997) *The Complete Pyramids: Solving the Ancient Mysteries.* London: Thames and Hudson.

34. Mark, J. J., 2009. "Giza." World History Encyclopedia. URL https://www.worldhistory.org/giza/ (accessed 11.1.22).

35. Mark, J.J., n.d. "The Seven Wonders." World History Encyclopedia. URL

https://www.worldhistory.org/The_Seven_Wonders/ (accessed 11.1.22).

36. Newton, C. T. (1857). *A History of Discoveries at Halicarnassus, Morea, Carthage and Tyre.* London, England: J. Murray.

37. Pausanias. (1978). *Description of Greece.* Cambridge, MA: Harvard University Press.

38. Pliny the Elder. (1977). *Natural History.* Cambridge: Harvard University Press.

39. Plutarch. *Lives of the Noble Grecians and Romans.*

40. Rush, J. (2021, February 3). Researchers Examine 1,900-Year-Old Mummy Without Opening It. Smithsonian Magazine. Retrieved from https://www.smithsonianmag.com/smart-news/researchers-examine-1900-year-old-mummy-without-opening-it-180976561/

41. Strabo. (2010). *Geography.* Oxford, England: Oxford University Press.

42. The British Museum. (n.d.). Mausoleum of Halikarnassos. Retrieved from https://www.britishmuseum.org/collection/galleries/mausoleum-halikarnassos

43. The Collector. (n.d.). Colossus of Rhodes: Ancient Wonder. Retrieved from https://www.thecollector.com/colossus-of-rhodes-ancient-wonder/

44. The Collector. (n.d.). The Statue of Zeus at Olympia: Wonder of the Ancient World. Retrieved from https://www.thecollector.com/statue-zeus-olympia/

45. The Past Magazine. (n.d.). The Changing Faces of Olympia. Retrieved from https://the-past.com/feature/the-changing-faces-of-olympia/

46. Verner, M. (2001). *The Pyramids: The Mystery, Culture, and Science of Egypt's Great Monuments.* New York: Grove Press.

47. Vitruvius. (1960). *The Ten Books on Architecture.* Cambridge, England: Cambridge University Press.

Printed in the USA
CPSIA information can be obtained
at www.ICGtesting.com
LVHW021730221123
764347LV00071B/933

9 781637 168646